Berta Hummel

Berta Hummel

Catalogue raisonné
1927–1931

Student days in Munich · Studienzeit in München

Prestel

Munich · Berlin · London · New York

Edited by the Berta-Hummel-Museum im Hummelhaus, Massing
Herausgegeben vom Berta-Hummel-Museum im Hummelhaus, Massing

Pictorial material has been kindly provided by the Berta-Hummel-Museum im Hummelhaus, Massing, with the exception of the following:
Kloster Sießen, p. 42, and the catalogue raisonné numbers KS A–R

The Library of Congress Cataloguing-in-Publication data is available

Die Bildvorlagen wurden freundlicherweise vom Berta-Hummel-Museum im Hummelhaus, Massing, zur Verfügung gestellt, außer:
Kloster Sießen, S. 42, sowie die Werkverzeichnisnummern KS A–R

Die Deutsche Bibliothek verzeichnet diese Publikation in der Deutschen Nationalbibliografie; detaillierte bibliografische Daten sind im Internet über http://dnb.ddb.de abrufbar

Prestel Verlag   Königinstraße 9   D-80539 Munich
Tel. +49 (0)89-38 17 09 0
Fax +49 (0)89-38 17 09 35
info@prestel.de
www.prestel.de

4 Bloomsbury Place   London WC1A 2QA
Tel. +44 (020) 7323-5004
Fax +44 (020) 7636-8004

175 Fifth Avenue   Suite 402   New York, NY 10010
Tel. +1 (212) 995-2720
Fax +1 (212) 995-2733

www.prestel.com

Prestel books are available worldwide. Please contact your nearest bookseller or one of the Prestel offices listed above for details concerning your local distributor.

Editing / Lektorat: Claudia Bauer
Design / Gestaltung: Verlagsservice G. Pfeifer, Germering
Cover design / Umschlag: Carolin Beck
Typesetting and lithography / Satz und Lithographie: EDV-Fotosatz Huber, Germering
Cover lithography / Lithographie Umschlag: ReproLine, München
Printing and binding / Druck und Bindung: Sellier, Freising

English translation / Übersetzung ins Englische: John W. Gabriel, Worpswede
Copyedited by Danko Szabó, Munich

Cover illustration / auf dem Umschlag
Front cover / Vorderseite:
Massing, cattle market / Massing, Viehmarkt
1931, crayon, pencil / Farbstift, Bleistift, 8 $\frac{1}{4}$ × 11 $\frac{1}{4}$ in. / 210 × 285 mm
HM 885A
Back cover / Rückseite:
Over the roofs / Über den Dächern
1928/30, watercolor / Aquarell, 9 $\frac{1}{2}$ × 15 $\frac{3}{4}$ in. / 235 × 400 mm
HM 352
* Druckstöcke vorhanden

Printed in Germany on acid-free paper

ISBN 3-7913-2824-7

Berta Hummel with "Lord," the family dog, 1930/31
Berta Hummel mit dem Hund »Lord«, 1930/31

Foreword
Vorwort

This volume illustrates the scope of Berta Hummel's creative powers during her student years in Munich—with the hitherto unpublished works of a well-known artist.

My heartfelt thanks go to Dr. Genoveva Nitz and Sister Witgard Erler OSF for their initial encouragement of my idea and, later, for their all-important collaboration in the planning and realization of this book.

Special thanks also go to Claudia Bauer, Renate Seemann, Karin Sohl, as well as to Andreas Huber and Florian Grüneklee for their competent assistance and work.

September 2002   *Alfred Hummel*

Der vorliegende Band zeigt das vielseitige Schaffen Berta Hummels während ihrer Münchener Studienzeit – die bisher unbekannten Werke einer bekannten Künstlerin.

Dr. Genoveva Nitz und Schwester Witgard Erler OSF haben mich zunächst in meiner Idee bestärkt und später dann entscheidend am Konzept und der Realisierung dieses Werkes mitgearbeitet. Ihnen gilt mein herzlicher Dank.

Für ihre kompetente Hilfe und Arbeit danke ich besonders Claudia Bauer, Renate Seemann, Karin Sohl sowie Andreas Huber und Florian Grüneklee.

September 2002   *Alfred Hummel*

The "Different" Berta Hummel

"The world's most beloved youngsters"—many would agree with this opinion about the "Hummel children," cited in a dictionary of caricature.[1] These porcelain figurines are ubiquitous, smiling out of show windows on busy shopping streets, airport shops and collectors' display cases around the world. At their public premiere in 1935 at the Leipzig Spring Fair, they already caused a wave of enthusiasm that soon grew to enormous proportions. In allusion to the name of their creator, the Franciscan nun Maria Innocentia Hummel, a bumblebee (German *Hummel*) was chosen as the figurines' trademark.[2]

Only in the past twenty years have people begun to look behind the trademark—with surprising results. The unknown oeuvre of an extremely well-known artist has come to light, a diverse range of imagery whose originality and inventiveness are a far cry from the best-of-all-possible-worlds cliché associated with the Hummel figurines. In a curious way, the work of Berta Hummel—Sister Maria Innocentia's baptismal name—has suffered a fate that parallels that of Wilhelm Busch, the famous German satirist. Both were ultimately victims of their own popularity, and the lifework of both was overshadowed by a single one of its facets.

The existence of a "different" Berta Hummel was pointed out as early as 1947, a year after the artist's death, by her former teacher, Else Brauneis. Brauneis, a professor at the Academy of Visual Arts in Munich, was referring to watercolors she had seen that year in a memorial exhibition in Massing.[3] Yet years were to pass before a review of Hummel's oeuvre brought to light about four hundred paintings and graphic works, done in the brief period of 1927 to 1931, as a student in Munich, before she took her vows. Their variety and astonishing technical mastery could not help but prompt a revision of the one-sided notion of her art conveyed by the commercial success of the Hummel figurines.

Berta Hummel was born on May 21, 1909, in Massing, Germany. The Hummels, a respected family of merchants that originated from the Württemberg region, had settled there in the nineteenth century, in what was then still a quiet, rural market town. The third oldest of seven children, Berta grew up in the sheltered atmosphere of a harmonious and devout family life. She had a precocious artistic gift, which was furthered especially by her father, Adolf Hummel. Berta was to remain grateful throughout her life for his support, which included permission to study art in Munich—something by no means usual for a young country girl at that time. In one of the first letters written in her freshman year at the School of Decorative Arts, she told her father, "I want to express [. . .] my heartfelt thanks to you for everything good you have already done for me. If only I could recompense through diligence what you have expended on me till now."[4] Even the later letters from Sießen Convent were still signed, "Your grateful child Bertl."

As a Student in Munich, 1927–31

Berta Hummel enrolled at the State School of Decorative Arts in Munich in the summer semester of 1927. In contrast to many other German cities, in Munich fine and applied arts were taught at separate institutions.[5] While fledgling freelancers attended the Academy of Visual Arts, future art teachers took instruction at the School of Decorative Arts at Luisenstrasse 37, which had been a state institution since 1868. On the occasion of the sixtieth anniversary of its founding in 1928, the school was rechristened State School of Applied Art. A further change in name, to Academy for Applied Art, followed in 1937. After the war the two Munich academies were amalgamated into the College, later Academy, of Visual Arts.

Interestingly, female students were not accepted into the academy until 1919. The School of Decorative Arts, in contrast, instituted a department for the "training of female drawing teachers" in 1872.[6] Its curriculum included "linear drawing with the requisite illustrations from geometry, ornamental drawing, figure drawing, floral drawing, the art of woodcut, art history, perspective, and shading."

Hummel child Katharina/Hummelkind Katharina
1923/25, watercolor, ink/Wasserfarbe, Tinte,
2 $\frac{1}{2}$ × 1 $\frac{3}{4}$ in./65 × 45 mm
HM 438

Instruction at the time of Berta Hummel's attendance was still largely based on this canon. Her surviving semester and examination certificates reflect a course range nearly identical to the nineteenth-century curriculum just outlined.[7] An obligation to traditional values was also evident in a lecture in art history by Dr. Hans Kiener, which Berta attended in the winter semester of 1930. Fortunately some of her lecture notes have survived, and they provide revealing insight into the art historian's approach. Similarly, the professors responsible for the practical side of Berta's training, Friedrich Wirnhier (1868–1952), Maximilian Dasio (1865–1954), and Else Brauneis (1877–1959), favored conservative styles as practicing artists. They regularly contributed to the exhibitions of the Munich Artists' Cooperative from 1929 to 1933. As late as 1937, when all "modernistic" tendencies were strictly banned, Wirnhier was still represented with paintings and drawings in the catalogues of the Great Munich Art Exhibition and the Annual Exhibition at the Neue Pinakothek.

Her student years in Munich were perhaps the happiest in Berta Hummel's short life. Her letters to family and friends abounded with enthusiastic descriptions of goings-on at the art school and proud reports of personal successes. The great energy with which she put her good intentions into practice, something already reflected in her elementary school report cards, developed in the heady atmosphere of college life into a tireless application to her work. Every accomplishment was a source of joy, every step forward opened new doors. For instance, she soon recognized the potential of printing techniques such as woodcut and lithography to reproduce her own drawings.[8] Her first year already saw Berta printing woodcuts with various motifs, which she regularly sent out as postcards and greeting cards.

Despite the fact that she was sometimes overcome by the feeling of "being only half out of my baby shoes,"[9] Berta was evidently very self-confident with regard to her work. She left Friedrich Wirnhier's class prematurely and enrolled in an advanced course with Maximilian Dasio. "Well," as she explained her decision in a letter, "Wirnhier was naturally very unpleasantly surprised. He just couldn't believe it, and thought I wouldn't be able to see anything more with Dasio, since I would be one of the very best there, too. In short, it was almost a little annoying that his very best pupil was leaving, the professor said, but it had to come sooner or later. I naturally feel very sorry about it, but it can't be changed; I have to consider my advantage. Wirnhier still wants me to bring my watercolors to him for correction, saying it would please him, so naturally I shall."[10] In another place she writes, "Wirnhier is proud to have discovered my talent, and he really means it, and why grudge him the pleasure; he says I had by far the best portfolio."[11]

Alongside his diverse activities as medallion designer, painter and graphic artist, Dasio was a committed teacher. On the faculty of the School of Decorative Arts from 1901, he was named ministerial counsel in the Bavarian State Ministry of Education and Culture in 1920. Even after retiring officially in April 1930, Dasio continued to head a class of teaching degree candidates. Apart from Else Brauneis, Dasio was the teacher Berta mentioned most frequently. She also portrayed him in two drawings, two watercolors and a woodcut (KS M, KS N, KS O, HM 157, HM 636). As she recalled one of these sessions: "I visited Herr Dasio in his studio today, and just imagine, he actually sat for me, cigar in mouth, reading the newspaper, and I really managed quite well, so he was very satisfied with the result, and Frau Brauneis praised me to the skies, saying it was the best thing I'd done. 'Come back any time you feel like it, I'm always here,' Herr Dasio told me afterwards, and I certainly shall take the opportunity; because it can do no harm and is an honor, too."[12] The traits of caricature in the woodcut version of this portrait (HM 636) may well have appealed to the professor's slightly bizarre sense of humor. Back in 1920, his younger colleague, Anton Marxmüller (1898–1984), had presented him with a delightful series of Dasio caricatures on his fifty-fifth birthday.[13]

Concurrently with the Dasio portraits two portrayals emerged—a graphite drawing and a deeply emotional close-up view in watercolor—of Else Brauneis, who had the closest relationship with Berta of any of the school's professors (KS L, HM 142a). Brauneis taught watercolor and the traditional disciplines of descriptive geometry, perspective and shading. She conducted the seminar for female drawing teachers and, as head of the library, had the task of interesting students in "various fields by changing displays of works/exhibitions of visual materials relating to individual fields, in connection with instruction in the various classes."[14]

In Professor Brauneis, a practicing Protestant, Berta had a strict yet understanding mentor who embodied a high work ethic. This was to reveal itself in an indicative way after the war. Despite illness and difficult living conditions, the seventy-year-old Brauneis undertook the two-hour journey on foot and by train to her post every morning, because she wanted to "contribute actively to building up our old academy."[15] Else Brauneis was very much concerned to further her students' careers. Even after Berta Hummel had entered the convent, she continued to offer her support in the form of advice and practical aid. As Berta recalled her farewell visit to Professor Brauneis: "I spent a long time with her—she is a noble person whom one cannot help but respect. She hopes to arrange her study trips so that I will be able to come along. I have never had a teacher like Frau Brauneis; and so it was truly hard for me to have to say farewell and leave Munich for good. [. . .] It is truly a sacrifice for me; but Sießen [Convent] provides me with a wonderful field of activity, where I can be active artistically as well as in the school; Frau Prof. Brauneis appreciates this, and curch textile design is one of the finest fields, in which she can be a great deal of help to me."[16]

While Berta was living at Sießen Convent, Else Brauneis arranged to have money sent to her from the sale of a drawing and a watercolor, and repeated her offer of help: "Are you satisfied with your work, and do you sometimes do your own art as well? Please don't neglect it, Bertl, and if you want to, send me some pieces now and then."[17] Then Brauneis goes on to remark on the lack of comradeship among the professors, shedding light on the increasingly uneasy political situation at the state school: "[. . .] we all just live alongside one another here and never with one another. The coldness sometimes makes one shiver."

Conflicts came to a head when Prof. Richard Klein, a man of National Socialist leanings, assumed the post of director. Prof. Fritz Helmuth Ehmcke, a graphic designer whose typography course Berta had taken as an elective, was denounced by Klein, among other reasons because he had "no affinity whatsoever with National Socialism," and lost his post.[18] In a later letter to Berta, Brauneis described the concatenation of external pressures and personal rancour that arose after the outbreak of war: "Many rooms at our school have been lost to a new emergency medical station— that's war. [. . .] But since our director requires grand reception rooms, and since his brother, despite the fact that he has no rights at our school, possesses his own large room, etc., the Herr Direktor explained to me that he had no space for the watercolor class, and I completed his sentence, 'and not the slightest interest in it, either.' This hurts me deeply—because there were many applications, and basically Prof. Klein has no idea of my work— nor what it means to bring something out of young people who only occasionally find time for the watercolor class *despite everything* [. . .]. It's sad— but great successes like Klein has—do not always improve a man. At any rate, the watercolor class is at the moment a "Volk ohne Raum" 'A Nation without Space,' the title of a then-popular nationalistic novel] and there is no good will to make space for it."[19]

Hummel child Viki/Hummelkind Viki
1923/25, watercolor, ink/Wasserfarbe, Tinte,
2 ¹/₂ × 1 ³/₄ in./65 × 45 mm
HM 439

Hummel must have suffered under the changed school atmosphere during her second sojourn in Munich in 1935–37. Her first study period seems not yet to have been affected by signs of growing Nazi influence, although she did note that "Dasio doesn't have much to say any more, unlike Prof. Klein, a very significant artist." Klein had introduced generally stricter grading, yet appreciated Hummel's talent, saying that "[. . .] only a single student was truly artistically gifted and really apt, and she was from Rottal and capable of development. Another prof. who would like to have me."[20] And a few days later: "I'm being besieged from all sides, every prof. would consider it a pleasure and honor to further my artistic career (Prof. Klein, Prof. Jaskolla—Brauneis, Pretorius—Kornmann, Prof. Kolb)."[21] Alluding to the old rivalry between the schools of fine and applied art, the same letter mentions an exhibition planned at the state school that "[. . .] is intended to show that women drawing teachers are capable of artistic achievement, too."

Hummel's Oeuvre

The carefreeness and peace of mind Hummel enjoyed during her first Munich years are reflected in a productive, diverse oeuvre encompassing landscapes, city views, floral studies, still lifes, portraits, pictures of children, caricatures, and decorative works. The techniques employed are equally diverse: woodcut and lithography, drawings in pencil, graphite, red chalk and charcoal, and paintings in watercolor and oils.

In 1928 Hummel began to concentrate increasingly on watercolor, which was well suited to her rapid, fluent painting style and fine sense of color. It was in this medium that she achieved the greatest artistic freedom. Paintings like "Girls in ethnic Costume" (HM 196a) and the study of the head of her dog "Lord" (HM 210) are pure colorism—the former an insouciant play with rapidly juxtaposed, strongly contrasting bands which gel into a figure, the latter a nearly monochrome, delicately nuanced harmony. The rigorous rhythms of "Above the Roofs" (HM 352), in contrast, reflect an essay on geometric abstraction. Seen from a bird's-eye view, the network of streets and roofs form a complex of intersecting diagonals. The same development towards abstraction is found in the conscious structuring of a market scene (HM 265), based on a stepwise arrangement of horizontal sequences clearly set off from one another in terms of both form and color. In compositions like these "the subject becomes unimportant, as if vanishing into an image that, as a self-contained construction of form and color, is sufficient unto itself."[22] In another work, a seemingly random excerpt, a view from an unexpected vantage point, suffices to evoke an idea of the whole object, a humble old house (HM 206).

Hummel child Centa/Hummelkind Centa
1923/25, watercolor, ink/Wasserfarbe, Tinte,
2 $^1/_2$ × 1 $^3/_4$ in./66 × 45 mm
HM 440

Unlike the few oils of the student period, which are virtually all faithful reflections of the motifs, Hummel's watercolors reflect an enjoyment of experiment and an interest in testing the many potentials of the medium. The majority are executed wet-in-wet, with the unpainted white paper ground forming the lightest value. The increasing brilliance of Hummel's works from 1928–30 is especially evident in her floral pieces. Her virtuosity in establishing an interplay between visual idea and technique is seen in "Lady in Red" (HM 239). The slender, lovely figure in a plain red dress exudes an immediate presence, despite the way she turns away as if musing about something that remains hidden to the outside world. The impression of secrecy and unapproachability evoked by the figure's pose is underscored by the fluidity and lucid transparency of the paint application. An increasing detachment from objective representation is reflected, in some cases, in a dissolution of the subject into flat paint areas, as in the portrait of Else Brauneis (HM 142a) and the quiet, altar-like interior (HM 868), and, in others, in hasty, liberated brushstrokes, as in the study of a farmer (HM 938a) or the rendering of an excursion boat party on Lake Chiem (HM 869).

After entering the convent, Hummel unfortunately largely abandoned watercolor in favor of pastels. A very few floral pieces, dating to her later Sießen years, were executed for the most part in "covering colors." These works lack the transparency and spontaneity of Hummel's watercolors in the classical wet-in-wet technique.

Comprising nearly eighty examples, the floral compositions represent the second largest group of works by the "different" Berta Hummel. It begins with sensitive pencil drawings that can be dated to the early semesters of 1927–28. With a precision recalling that of botanical illustrations, these drawings often depict the various stages in the life of a plant, from budding and full blossom to wilting and fading. The experience gained through such careful observation provided the basis for the freer approach of the 1928–30 watercolors, which live and breathe pure color. Strong contrasts are used to accentuate the magnificent palette of such compositions as (HM 221b or HM 523). A different approach is seen in the subtle gradations of "Chrysanthemum" (HM 333) or the fleeting, delicate strokes in (HM 311), which evoke the fragile beauty and transitory life of flowers.

Hummel child Berta/Hummelkind Berta
1923/25, watercolor, ink/Wasserfarbe, Tinte,
2 ¹/₂ × 2 in./66 × 50 mm
HM 441

There is a comparatively late statement by the artist that seems to shed light on the difference between her painstaking, naturalistic pencil drawings and the open, liberated nature of her watercolors. It dates to her second study period in Munich, and was made in reply to her brother Franz's questions about painting. Writing to him on June 9, 1936, Maria Innocentia put her artistic credo in a nutshell: "Take a little flower, a blade of grass, look at it closely, compare how different and manifold their shapes are, then go home and draw what you have observed and seen. You will see how necessary it is to first learn to really *see*, but then also how important it is to capture the essence. Such as the helpless wavering of a blade of grass, the stiffness and bristling of underbrush, the 'silent blooming' of a violet—or better, from the animal realm—the essence of an eagle as opposed to that of a dove. [. . .] The most important thing is not that you correctly and precisely *copy* something, but that you capture its essence, project yourself into it and then attempt to express it. [. . .] You should derive benefit from this, not incomprehensibility and untruthfulness, because when you do something you don't understand, it's not *true*. [. . .] Accustom yourself to being honest and leaving nothing up to chance, to making every stroke consciously. Just as nothing in nature is unrelated, every stroke must have a relation to the whole; for instance, a tree, its trunk, limbs, branches, leaves relate to one another, one emerges from the other. You must make a habit of drawing rightly, as growth teaches you—that is, no subordinate things before the main thing is there—not the eyes, nose and highlights on them before the head is there—not the feathers first before the bird is there. These are the main beginners' mistakes, and most people never get over them, partly because they were not taught to, or because they have been prevented by a lack of persistence."

Hummel's landscapes and cityscapes belong without exception to the period of her attendance at the Munich School of Decorative Arts. The great majority of these were done between 1928 and 1930, followed by a few examples from her second study period in 1935–36. Hummel enjoyed depicting subjects of this kind. She later regretted that life in the convent precluded it, saying: "Sometimes I really do feel the urge to paint in the narrow lanes and hidden corners as before, which one cannot well do as a nun."²³ The range of her approaches is reflected in four surviving watercolor views of Munich that capture the manifold charms of the big city. These extend from finely articulated, almost nervous detailing in the view over jumbled rooftops (HM 852) to rigorous, structural reduction in (HM 265), from a colorful complex of interlocking houses in the popular Au district (HM 863a) to the limited color range and resulting spaciousness of a view of stately "Ludwigstrasse" (HM 942). Several views of Salzburg, made during study excursions, have also survived. Such excursions to Lindau and Salzburg, where Hummel stayed up in the fortress, are mentioned in letters by

Portrait of Lotte Angslperger
Porträt Lotte Anglsperger
1926, pencil/Bleistift,
7 ¹/₂ × 6 in./193 × 155 mm
HM 57

Else Brauneis. Also dating to about this time are mountain landscapes executed in the Salzburg region and around Lake Chiem. A further group of pictures, characterized by a brilliant palette, are devoted to studies of forests and trees.

A key place in her work is held by depictions of Hummel's birthplace, Massing. A deep affection for the town, reflected again and again in her work, had already been developed in her childhood. Painting excursions with her father and sister Centa (Kreszentia) awakened an interest in and sensitivity to the specific character of the Rottal region. During later school vacations spent at home, Hummel saw familiar things with fresh eyes. Her approximately fifty views of Massing and environs were introduced by a series of woodcuts and ink drawings, including a charmingly playful "Market Scene" with the house where Berta was born in the background (HM 623). Great skill is evident in the contrast between the light, expansive planes of the background and the dark, vivacious foreground scene with small figures that appear to be dancing. Motifs make their appearance here that would later form the repertoire of the typical "Hummel pictures," and would still be found in the very last works, the drawings posthumously published under the title "Letztes Schenken" (Final Bequest); for instance, the gossiping farm people with overlarge feet and huge umbrellas.

The Hummels' house stood at the eastern end of the marketplace, a vantage point from which Berta could observe the colorful activity at the stalls (HM 486, HM 46). Yet she also knew the busy square as a place of Christmas tranquillity (HM 618) and in the calm of early morning, where, as if in a dream, a horse patiently waits in front of its wagon for the day's activity to begin (HM 651). The same atmosphere of tranquil reverie suffuses the view into the street leading past the Hummels' house into the marketplace—now Berta-Hummel-Strasse—with its expanses of amorphous shadow forming a contrast to the row of houses (HM 652). Since many of the old tradesmens' houses have long since been torn down and the appearance of the area has been fundamentally altered by a modern street network, Hummel's depictions, beyond their aesthetic statement, possess great significance as documents of local history, especially as a considerable number of her depictions of Massing and environs are precisely dated. Hummel also recorded local life and customs—a "Corpus Christi Procession" (HM 498), a night watchman (HM 649) making his rounds, people haggling at the "Cattle Market" (Hm 858A), or a shoemaker quietly at work in his shop (HM 644, HM 645).

Hummel's affection for her home town became especially apparent in her choice of the subject of Massing for the gift presented to her parents on their silver wedding anniversary. In this large appliqué wall hanging she arranged town landmarks and motifs from farming life in a collage-like way—not as a realistic view of the town but, so to speak, an idealized summing up of the world she was soon to leave in order to begin a new life at Sießen Convent (HM 493B).

The impressions and experiences of her previous life were not so easily forgotten. In the compositions with favorite childrens' subjects done at the convent, a range of remembered motifs continually recur. Certain objects appear in stylized form, inserted like theater props into new contexts—the picket fence seen in many views of Massing, the fir tree, the Marterl shrine by a path through the fields, the serene river valley, and the gently rolling hills of the Rottal landscape. The "Hummel pictures," as idealized as they sometimes seem, could only have been done on the basis of real, lived experiences.

At the beginning of a series of portraits stand several portraits of Berta's family and relatives. These are supplemented by depictions of acquaintances, studies of farming life, and works done from models at the state school. Two self-portraits reveal the way Berta saw herself during these years. The first, a pencil drawing of 1928 (HM 432), is dominated by the penetrating, critical gaze of the nineteen-year-old girl. The eyes are still the predominant features in the second portrait, in red chalk, done the following year (HM 514), yet here their expression is more reserved, almost even vulnerable. The extensive group of portraits attests to the frankness with which the young Berta Hummel approached her environment. To all, whether friends or professional models, she brought the same empathy, in an attempt to transcend a mere record of physiognomical traits and capture her sitters in all the complexity of their personality.

As early as the art school entrance examination, Hummel found herself confronted with a theme that, while a familiar part of the big-city scene in the late 1920s, must have seemed new and alien to someone accustomed to the sheltered life of a prosperous small-town fami-ly. As she reported in a letter of June 12, 1927, she was given the assignment of "drawing a completely emaciated man."[24] Although the technical task involved working out bone struc-ture, the subject of the assignment was oppressively up to date—one did not have to look far to find signs of the widespread poverty of the day, as they appeared with shocking directness, for instance, in the imagery of Käthe Kollwitz.

As regards technique, Hummel's portraits represent the most diverse group of all. She worked in pen and ink, pencil, red chalk and pastel, and later principally in watercolor and charcoal. The watercolors encompass such different subjects as the elegant costume study of "Lady in Blue" (HM 243), the strikingly characterized heads of HM 149a and HM 156, and a few children's portraits (HM 128, HM 214, HM 238). The latter are portraits in the true sense, a far cry from the schematic cuteness of the Hummel figurines. The little boy lost in contemplation of a picture book (HM 50) or the girl looking insecurely aside (HM 236) are observed with the same insight and seriousness as Hummel's adult sitters.

It was in the charcoal drawings that she achieved the greatest force of expression. A famil-iarity with Expressionist portraiture is reflected in depictions of Margret, an elderly model em-ployed at the art school. Berta, apparently fascinated by her bizarre appearance, portrayed her several times—the sunken cheeks, tired, dull eyes, and nearly toothless mouth with swollen lower lip (HM 147, HM 148, HM 200, KS P, KS Q, KS R). It is an interesting fact that the most penetrating portraits of the artist known for her cheerful "Hummel children" were devoted to the subject of aging. With deep empathy yet without false pathos, she registered the disillu-sionment and resignation of elderly people, the weakness of an emaciated old man on the brink of death (HM 229), and the quiet dignity of an old farmwoman reading her prayer book (HM 198).

Very few of Hummel's caricatures have survived. It is very likely that she produced a large number during her student years, because according to notes by Sister Maria Laura Brugger, a fellow-student at the state school and later custodian of that part of her artistic estate kept at Sießen Convent, Hummel "used to capture the characteristic appearance of Professor Dasio in various caricatures."[25] When one such sketch was found by chance in a wastepaper basket, Berta was immediately suspected: "Frau Professor Else Brauneis recognized the brilliant touch right off [. . .] and said smilingly: 'This could have been only one person—that scamp of a girl in Dasio's class.' Dasio himself heard about it, and said, without the slightest trace of irritability: 'You tell that scamp of a girl that she should have gone ahead and pulled the drawer out farther.' (By drawer he meant his habitually protruding lower lip.)"[26]

Two New Year's greeting cards for 1930 (HM 65, HM 846) were publi-shed in the first edition of the *Hummel-Buch* in 1934. Seen from a "Drun-ken Perspective" (HM 846), the finely delineated stairways and tall build-ings of a big city begin to totter. In designing a signet for the quart beer jugs featured at the Hofbräuhaus, the artist needed only transpose her own initials, "B.H.," to HB. Similarly, Berta was not adverse to poking fun at country folk (HM 192, HM 193). Her group of three gossiping women is a marvel of individual characterization: one, overly plump, with billow-ing umbrella to match; her bespectacled companion bursting with the latest news; and a third, thin, malicious woman with tight-pressed lips and pointed chin, a predecessor of Hummel's later witchlike figures. She had just as sharp an eye for the failings of men, whom she depicted as per-sonifications of stupidity, deviousness or vanity. The same figures shown angrily haggling at the "Cattle Market" trot hypocritically along in the

Portrait of Maria Anglsperger
Porträt Maria Anglsperger
1926, pencil/Bleistift,
8 1/4 × 6 in./210 × 152 mm
HM 56

"Corpus Christi Procession" (HM 885A, HM 886). In emphasizing the comical aspects of a roughhouse between two boys (HM 64) Hummel inadvertently created a prototype for her later Hummel figurines. Some of the most famous of these depictions of children in fact verge on caricature, such as the precisely depicted situations in the "Occupations" series in which children more or less successfully attempt to imitate the activities of adults, or the pair representing "Painter" and "Art Critic", a humorous quintessence distilled from Hummel's own experiences in the field.

Works of applied art in the narrower sense have also survived from her first years at the School of Decorative Art. These include designs for "Children's Wallpaper" (HM 16-19) and a mitten (HM 469). For an unspecified "Study" made in her freshman year for the Stabilo Company, Hummel received an advance.[27] Designs for gingerbread were also part of the métier; Dasio is known to have produced such designs for the Ebenböck Company in 1898–99.[28] Hummel's design shows "Hansel and Gretel at the Witch's House" (KS). In 1929, for the family business, she created elaborate display-window decorations for Easter and Christmas (HM 453, HM 448), and a company symbol featuring a stylized bee. This pun on her family name always amused her. As a young girl she had portrayed herself and her siblings as bumblebees in a delightful series of miniature character studies, and even her late work featured the motif of a flying bumblebee as a kind of pictographic signature.

Taking the Veil

After she entered the Franciscan Convent at Sießen on April 22, 1931, at the age of only twenty-two, the focus of Hummel's art shifted in terms of subject matter, technique and style. Her previous subjects had to make way for the tasks assigned her at the convent. These were many and various: work in the highly regarded vestment workshop (whose artistic direction she would assume in 1934); drawing instruction at St. Anna School in Saulgau; the execution of altar paintings and small-format devotional images for the publishing houses Ver Sacrum (Rottenburg), Emil Fink (Stuttgart), Ars Sacra, and the Gesellschaft für christliche Kunst (Munich); and above all, designs for her "Hummel children" cards.

Her investiture as a nun took place in August 1933. Berta received the name Maria Innocentia, and from that point on often signed her works "M.I. Hummel." The publication of the *Hummel-Buch* in 1934, with Emil Fink Verlag, Stuttgart, led to a marked increase in Maria Innocentia's popularity. In reaction to the book's success, Dr. Michael Buchberger, Bishop of Regensburg, noted that it had "struck the popular soul."[29] At the same time, the art-loving Buchberger recognized the latent risk of artistic limitation, saying that Sister Maria Innocentia needed "[. . .] a great and serious task in order to grow intellectually, spiritually and artistically by applying herself to it."[30] He invited her to illustrate a planned school Bible. Hummel agreed, but had to recant when the convent administration prohibited her involvement in the Bible project[31] and acceded to a request by the Goebel Porcelain Company that her "Hummel children" cards be translated into three-dimensional form. Maria Innocentia had her doubts, but finally agreed to take on the task. To her it was principally a question of artistic conscience whether her compositions could survive translation into three-dimensional terms, whether the nuanced lineatures of charcoal drawings could be recast into plastic form without a loss of quality. The figurines she finally designed proved immensely successful. Yet they also faced Maria Innocentia with the harsh laws of marketing. The obligation to produce continually new children's motifs meant abandoning other subject matter—cityscapes and landscapes disappeared from her work, floral pictures grew seldom, the portraits often appeared hasty and schematic.

In turn, the new tasks at the convent demanded a concentration on new techniques. Berta had looked forward to the vestment workshop, and began working there just a day after her arrival at Sießen. Her Massing wall hanging had already provided an opportunity to probe the possibilities of textile work. Her achievements in this field at the state school had attracted the interest of the textile specialist Professor Else Jaskolla, whom she mentions in the above cited letter[32] as one of the instructors who would have been happy to further her career. An early design for a "Chasuble" (HM 565) dates back to her student days. Two small-format depictions of the Madonna (HM 70, HM 71), done at about the time she entered the convent, represent early practice studies that reflect an involvement with the specific, planar aspects of parament design. The printing processes used to reproduce both her devotional and the Hummel card designs were also a source of concern, for "[. . .] it is very important for me to know the reproduction process so that I can take technical difficulties into account when working."[33] In an attempt to anticipate the demands of printing, Hummel soon adopted the medium of pastel. The great majority of the children's pictures intended for reproduction were executed as pastel and charcoal drawings. In the case of altar paintings, on the other hand, oils were preferred. The designs for these were supplied in gouache, tempera and mixed techniques.

Under the compulsions of contract work, Maria Innocentia was forced to the bitter realization that her goals as an artist could not be reconciled with her duties as a nun. The correspondence concerning the failed Bible project conveys a sad picture of her discouragement and self-doubt during related negotiations in Munich.[34] A convent administration with a better understanding of her seriousness as an artist would not have remained impervious to signs of her agonizing inward conflict. Yet she was destined to face it alone—and to sublimate it in perhaps the only way she knew how, in a magnificent Stations of the Cross, begun in 1936. About fifty sketches for this work have survived, some now at Sießen Covent, others at the Berta Hummel Museum in Massing.

This dark, expressionistic sequence was the most personal work Maria Innocentia Hummel produced during these years, a last flaring-up of an individual artistic volition that made no concessions to the notion of an Age of Innocence regained. It was the logical continuation of the path she had taken with the final charcoal portraits of her art school years. Yet Maria Innocentia was not to be permitted—or would not permit herself—to walk this path any farther. Her understanding of life in a religious order demanded that she voluntarily put her efforts in the service of others. Her final years would be largely devoted to contract projects. On November 6, 1946, at the age of only thirty-seven, Sister Maria Innocentia Hummel died of tuberculosis at Sießen.

Notes

1 Kurt Flemig, Karikaturisten-Lexikon, Munich, New Providence et al., 1993, p. 128.

2 The Hummel figurines were not modelled by Maria Innocentia herself, but were produced on the basis of her designs by modellers of the W. Goebel Porzellanfabrik.

3 "Seeing her watercolors again gave me great pleasure, and they reflect the other, then so cheerful Bertel Hummel." Letter from Else Brauneis to Adolf Hummel, September 9, 1947, Berta Hummel Museum Massing (BHM Massing).

4 Letter of June 15, 1927, BHM Massing.

5 Winfried Nerdinger, "Fatale Kontinuität," in Thomas Zacharias (ed.), Tradition und Widerspruch – 175 Jahre Kunstakademie München, Munich, 1985, p. 54: "Whereas schools of applied art and academies, based on the model of the Weimar Bauhaus, were integrated in Berlin, Karlsruhe, Breslau and Stuttgart as well, Munich continued to insist on a strict separation of fine and applied art."

6 On the history of the Kunstgewerbeschule, see Wolfgang Kehr, "Kunsterzieher an der Akademie," in ibid., p. 287 ff.

7 In her certificate of the "Lehramtsprüfung für Zeichenlehrerinnen" (Final Examination for Female Drawing Teachers), dated March 18, 1931, grades are given on the following subjects: "projection drawing, perspective drawing, ornamental drawing, figure drawing: head model drawn from life, figure drawing: draped figure from life, flower drawing from nature, colored depiction from nature, design of an ornament, teaching practice and methodology of drawing instruction, art history, styles in art." Her attendance of courses in woodcut (with the xylographer Albert Fallscheer), lithography (with Bartholomäus Neumeier), watercolor and descriptive geometry (with Prof. Else Brauneis) is confirmed in semester report cards.

8 Letter to a girlfriend, June 12, 1927, photocopy in BHM Massing.

9 Letter from Else Brauneis, October 26, 1931, BHM Massing.

10 Letter of October 7, 1928, BHM Massing.

11 Letter of November 14, 1931, BHM Massing.

12 Letter of January 15, 1930, BHM Massing.

13 Ingrid S. Weber, Maximilian Dasio 1865–1954. Münchner Maler, Medailleur und Ministerialrat, exh. cat., Munich, 1985, p. 180 f.

14 Staatliche Kunstgewerbeschule München. Excerpt from statutes and curriculum, n.d. (probably c. 1927), p. 15.

15 Letter from Else Brauneis to Adolf Hummel, May 1, 1947, BHM Massing.

16 Letter of March 20, 1931, BHM Massing.

17 Letter of Else Brauneis, October 26, 1931. "I want to send you cordial greetings – and 80 marks for the sale of a pencil drawing 'Weather Moods' and a watercolor 'Harbor in Lindau' [. . .] The watercolor (50 M) and the drawing (30 M) were purchased by Director Beck of Rupprechtstrasse. I once came across him truly enthusing about the watercolor show I had made of my class, and where your works were probably the highlight", Sießen Convent.

18 Thomas Zacharias, (Art) reine Kunst. Die Münchener Akademie um 1937, Munich, 1987, p. 10.

19 Letter of December 11, 1939, BHM Massing.

20 Letter of March 14, 1931, BHM Massing.

21 Letter of March 20, 1931, BHM Massing.

22 Martin Ortmeier, "Das andere Werk der Berta Hummel," in: Die andere Berta Hummel. Unbekannte Werke einer bekannten Künstlerin, exh. cat., Regensburg, 1986, p. 21.

23 Letter of July 15, 1938, BHM Massing.

24 Letter of June 12, 1927, copy in BHM Massing.

25 Written communication from Sister M. Witgard Erler, Sießen Convent.

26 Ibid.

27 Postcard of December 18, 1927, BHM Massing.

28 Ingrid S. Weber, op. cit., p. 20.

29 Letter of December 29, 1934, from Bishop Buchberger to the publishers Josef Kösel and Friedrich Pustet, Bischöfliches Zentralarchiv, Regensburg.

30 Letter of December 29, 1934, from Bishop Buchberger to the Hummel family, BHM Massing.

31 See letters from Bishop Buchberger to Sister Innocentia Hummel, December 3, 1934, and to Sießen Convent, April 12, 1935, Sießen Convent.

32 Letter of March 20, 1931, BHM Massing.

33 Letter of May 22, 1933, BHM Massing.

34 Letter of July 11, 1935, from Publisher Josef Kösel and Friedrich Pustet to Bishop Buchberger, Bischöfliches Zentralarchiv, Regensburg.

"Hummel Bertl, Draw Me!"
Centa remembers her sister Berta

Berta Hummel had an especially close relationship with her sister Kreszentia, known as Centa, who was two years younger. In addition to shared school years, their tie was deepened by holidays spent together and Centa's repeated visits to Munich, and later to Sießen Convent. Centa Hummel, who now lives in Passau, still has vivid recollections of the period. Claudia Bauer spoke with her.

Your father, Adolf Hummel, actually wanted to become a sculptor, and later, after adopting a business career, he still retained a strong interest in cultural affairs. Did your sister Berta's artistic talent lie in the family?

Actually both of our parents were very musical people, but it is true that our father, especially, had a strong artistic vein. He was the only son in the family, so despite his desire to become a sculptor he had to take over the grocery established by his father, Jakob Hummel, in Massing. In addition to running his business he also served as mayor, wrote a local history of Massing, and was later made honorary freeman of the city. Although his business made great demands on him, he often used to sit down evenings and pursue his hobbies, for instance, decorating little wooden boxes with pokerwork designs, as presents for his wife. We children were allowed to watch him doing this and enjoyed it tremendously.

Berta and Centa in their garden, Whitsun 1922
Berta und Centa im Garten, Pfingsten 1922

On our mother's side there was also an artist—her sister, our aunt, who painted in oils. Nor was our mother untalented, as I mentioned, but helping in the shop and caring for our family left her no time to be really active. All of us children were artistically quite versed. I had an especially deep relationship with Berta, and at the beginning of our school years she continually tried to convince me to go to the college of applied arts. At the time, Berta was still planning to become a gymnastics teacher.

When did Berta decide to adopt a career in art?

I enrolled in the Higher School for Girls in Simbach two years after Berta, and her decision was probably made shortly after that. For a long time Berta vacillated between the idea of becoming a gym teacher and training in art. The fact that I was better at athletics probably helped tip the scales. In the end I became a gym teacher, you know, and she went to art school.

Berta's great talent became apparent at an early age. Was she furthered at school and in your family?

At Massing Elementary School Berta was already something of a "little celebrity"—everybody knew her and admired her skills. "Hummel Bertl, draw me!" her schoolmates used always to beg her, and their voices still echo in my ears today. At the Higher School for Girls in Simbach, Berta was allowed to use the art room outside regular instruction hours, which was quite a privilege. One of the things she did back then was the oil painting "Sailing Ship."

Theater sketch performed by Berta and Centa at the wedding of their sister Katharina, 1932
Theaterspiel von Berta und Centa beim Hochzeitsfest ihrer Schwester Katharina, 1932

The family's goodwill came out especially in the fact that they paved the way for Berta to attend the Munich College of Decorative Art and supported her in every respect. At the time it was absolutely exceptional for a country girl to begin an education of this kind in Munich. Our father believed implicitly in Berta, and he even accompanied her to Munich for the entrance examination. She passed the exam as one of the best without specially preparing for it; she truly played it by ear. She later told me that one of the assignments consisted in drawing a man as he walked back and forth in front of the applicants.

The first period in Munich wasn't always easy for Berta. You were in close contact with your sister. Did she tell you about the initial difficulties she faced?

The problems Berta initially had in Munich were really related to external conditions rather than to her college studies. Her first landlady made life quite hard for her. Berta didn't feel comfortable in her room. Then too, she spent all her money on paints and usually didn't have enough left over to buy something to eat. Eventually Berta met two lay-sisters from Sießen Convent who were also attending the college, and they helped her find a room in a sisters' dormitory on Blumenstrasse. From then on her college days were very harmonious, and I can still remember that she often went to see exhibitions and enjoyed the cultural life very much.

Berta usually spent her vacations in Massing with the family. What reminiscences do you have of her from those days?

Staying with the family during vacations was surely an important and wonderful relief from her studies in Munich. Yet even during this leisure time Berta painted and drew a lot. When she came home from Munich, hardly a quarter of an hour would pass before Father would say, "Listen, Berta, I've got another fine character head for you, I'll drive you over there." This was how her many portrait studies of farmers and farmwomen from the countryside around Massing came about. Our dog "Lord," a boxer, also interested her; they had a very affectionate relationship. This is reflected in his frequent appearance in her works of this period.

I also have fond memories of the wonderful decorations Berta designed together with Father for the store—there were witches' huts, a mill that actually worked, and much more. Especially at Christmas time the two of them would always plan and make a display; Father was very inventive in this respect. Crowds of children used to gather outside the window and press their noses up against the glass. Numerous works with landscape motifs also emerged during vacations. Berta's pictures give you a good impression of how Massing and the surrounding villages looked back then—hardly any photographs exist, you know. Berta often took me along, and I would watch her painting or occupy myself with embroideries. She usually tried to encourage me to paint, too. "Look, Centa, this is how a painting develops [...]" she used to say on such occasions. Once, when we were visiting an aunt in the Palatinate, I actually did paint a castle ruin. But in the end I didn't have the courage to show it to her.

At what point did Berta's desire to enter the convent become apparent? Were you aware of the process that led to her decision?

The two lay-sisters from Sießen I told you about entered the Munich School of Decorative Arts later than Berta, and her professor, Maximilian Dasio, asked her to take care of the new arrivals as a prefect. I am sure that this close contact helped familiarize Berta with convent life. Berta never spoke about her actual decision to enter the convent; she just kept silent counsel with herself. The family accepted her step without much discussion. It was different at her school in Munich. After her final exam—which, by the way, she passed at the top of the class—Prof. Dasio offered her a position as instructor, but Berta declined because she had already decided for the convent. Dasio was deeply disappointed about this and turned away from Berta, although, as we later heard, he kept very precise track of her subsequent career, if without ever attempting to get in personal contact with her again. Prof. Else Brauneis, who also thought very highly of Berta, dealt with the situation quite differently. She continued to support Berta and did not break off their relationship, either.

Your family has very conscientiously collected and managed Berta's oeuvre. Was your father once again the driving force in this respect?

Definitely! Our father was a passionate collector in general, and had a reputation as such in Massing. Whenever anyone found anything interesting, be it old weapons or a mammoth tusk, they always said, "Take it to Hummel!" It was the same with Berta's drawings and paintings. From the first postcard she painted, he preserved everything, really every sheet, kept the things together after her death, and thus laid the groundwork for the present collection. The following generations continued to devote themselves to her works, until they finally found their place in the museum established expressly for the purpose. For us today it is especially important to show the countless admirers of the Hummel figures this largely unknown side of Berta Hummel.

In conclusion, could you tell us something about your sister's personality? What kind of a person was she, and how do you remember her?

Berta was a very positive, life-accepting and temperamental, almost impetuous person. She loved children above all else, as her work clearly reflects, and had a special sense of humor, which came out, for instance, in her caricatures. She had a very quick perception and went right to the crux in her drawings and paintings—especially the portraits—and had the ability to precisely capture a certain character or a certain atmosphere. This is a gift that is very rare, and one which I immeasurably admired in her.

Berta Hummel
Her Life

May 21, 1909
Berta Hummel is born in Massing an der Rott, Lower Bavaria, Germany

May 1, 1915
Starts at Massing Primary School

May 3, 1921
Moves up to the Marienhöhe Institute in Simbach am Inn, a secondary school for girls run by the Institute of the Blessed Virgin Mary

March 25, 1926
Finishes schooling at the Marienhöhe Institute

1927–31
Studies at the School of Decorative Arts in Munich (renamed in 1928 the State School of Applied Art) under Professors Maximilian

Dasio, Else Brauneis, Friedrich Wirnhier, and others; friendship with two young Franciscan nuns from Sießen Convent near Saulgau in Württemberg, who were also studying in Munich

March 18, 1931
Graduates from the State School of Applied Art in Munich with the highest grade (Grade A)

April 22, 1931
Enters the Franciscan convent in Sießen; works mainly in the vestment workshop and as a drawing teacher; paints children's pictures and commission work

From 1931 onward
Annual exhibitions in Sießen, Beuron, and Munich

As a student in Munich. Prof. Else Brauneis (front row, middle), Berta Hummel (second row, left, behind Sister M. Laura Brugger), Prof. Maximilian Dasio (back row, middle), 1931
Studienzeit in München. Prof. Else Brauneis (1. Reihe Mitte), Berta Hummel (2. Reihe links hinter Sr. M. Laura Brugger), Prof. Maximilian Dasio (letzte Reihe Mitte), 1931

December 1932
First edition of pictures and postcards in Rottenburg and Munich

May 30–June 8, 1933
Final visit to parental home prior to her investiture at Sießen Convent

August 22, 1933
Investiture; received the name Maria Innocentia; starts one-year novitiate

From 1933 onward
Permanent exhibition in the "Hummel-Room," Sießen Convent

August 30, 1934
First profession acceptance of first vows at a public mass

November 4, 1934
Publication of the first "Hummel Book" by Emil Fink Verlag, Stuttgart, in an edition of 5,000

1934/35
First cooperation with the W. Goebel Porzellanfabrik in Oeslau, today Rödental, near Coburg; production of first "Hummel figurines"

1935
First exhibition of Hummel figures at the Leipzig Spring Fair

May 5, 1935
Start of advanced studies at the State School of Applied Art in Munich

August 18–20, 1936
Visits the Porzellanfabrik Goebel in Oeslau; workers thank Sister Maria Innocentia for providing employment through the production of Hummel figurines

March 23, 1937
National Socialists attack Sister Maria Innocentia's children's pictures in the journal "The SA Man"

April 24, 1937
After interruption due to ill health, completes advanced studies at the State School of Applied Art in Munich, again with the highest grade

August 30, 1937
Professes eternal faith by taking her final vows

April 9, 1938
Arrival of the altarpiece for Massing, depicting Brother Konrad of Parzham, displayed at the left side altar in the parish church

October 1939
Publication of the second Hummel Book "Hui, die Hummel" by Ars sacra Verlag Josef Müller, Munich

November 4, 1940
Evacuation of Sießen Convent by order of the National Socialists

November 1940 and October 1942
Visits her parents in Massing to recuperate from her illness

August 1944–September 1945
Receives treatment in sanatoriums in Isny and Wangen

September 9, 1946
Returns to Sießen Convent

November 6, 1946
Sister Maria Innocentia Berta Hummel dies of tuberculosis at Sießen Convent

Berta Hummel at school in Simbach, 1926
Berta Hummel in Marienhöhe, Simbach, 1926

November 9, 1946
Burial in the Convent Cemetery in Sießen

August 20–24, 1947
Exhibition of works of Sister Maria Innocentia in the Anglsperger Inn in Massing

April 17–25, 1948
Exhibition in Friedrichshafen on Lake Constance of works by Sister Maria Innocentia Hummel

October 1950
Exhibition of Hummel pictures and Hummel figurines together with the A. Hummel Collection in Massing

1978
Opening of the present Hummel Room in Sießen Convent with children's pictures, altarpieces and sketches for "The Stations of the Cross"

1978
Opening of the Berta Hummel Museum in Massing; large collection of old and new Hummel figurines

1980–82
Touring exhibition through various cities in the USA entitled: "Formation of an Artist," displaying early works by Berta Hummel

July–October 1985
Fifty years of Maria Innocentia Hummel's figurines, 1935–85 at the Museum of the German Porcelain Industry, Hohenberg a. d. Eger

August 1985
"The Other Berta Hummel" Exhibition on the occasion of the opening of the Berta Hummel Primary School in Massing

November 6, 1986–February 1, 1987
Exhibition in the Diocesan Museum of Regensburg "The Other Berta Hummel – Unknown Works by a well known Artist"

October 1993
Opening of the Hummel Museum in New Braunfels, Texas, USA

Berta Hummel working on her first large format oil-painting, 1926/27
Berta Hummel vor ihrem ersten Ölbild, 1926/27

July 22, 1994
Inauguration of the new "Berta-Hummel-Museum im Hummelhaus" (in the building where she was born) in Massing

November 6, 1996
Fiftieth anniversary of Berta Hummel's death; opening of the exhibition "Last Gifts" in the Berta-Hummel-Museum im Hummelhaus in Massing

May 21, 1999
Ninetieth anniversary of the birth of Berta Hummel; opening of the exhibition "Cheerful Beginning" in Massing

June 27, 2000
Opening of the exhibition "Massing and Berta Hummel" in Massing on the occasion of the town's 650th anniversary of being granted its market privileges, as well as the Hummel family's 125th anniversary in Massing

June 27, 2001
Opening of the Commemorative exhibition "Hue of Remembrance," commemorating Maria Hummel (1951–1998), the founder of the Berta-Hummel-Museum im Hummelhaus in Massing

June 4, 2002
Opening of the exhibition "New Discoveries and New Acquisitions" in the Berta-Hummel-Museum im Hummelhaus in Massing

Berta with "Lord," at the window Franz Hummel, 1926/27
Berta mit »Lord«, am Fenster Franz Hummel, 1926/27

Die »andere« Berta Hummel

»Der Welt meistgeliebte Kinder« – so zitiert Kurt Flemig in seinem Karikaturisten-Lexikon[1] eine gängige Beschreibung der »Hummelfiguren«. Man trifft sie in aller Welt, sei es in Schaufenstern belebter Einkaufsstraßen, Flughafenläden oder Sammlervitrinen. Schon bei ihrer ersten Präsentation auf der Leipziger Frühjahrsmesse 1935 lösten sie eine Welle der Begeisterung aus, die mit der Zeit mehr und mehr anwuchs. Als Markenzeichen für die Figuren wurde eine Hummel verwendet – eine Anspielung auf den Namen ihrer Schöpferin, Schwester Maria Innocentia Hummel.[2]

Erst in den letzten zwanzig Jahren begann man, hinter das Markenzeichen zu schauen – mit überraschendem Resultat. Zum Vorschein gekommen ist das unbekannte Werk einer bekannten Künstlerin, das in seiner Offenheit und seinem Facettenreichtum denkbar weit entfernt von der schablonenhaften »heilen Welt« der beliebten »Hummelkinder« liegt. Das Schaffen der Berta Hummel – wie Schwester Maria Innocentia mit Taufnamen hieß – hat ein Schicksal erlitten, das eine Parallele bei Wilhelm Busch findet: Beide wurden letztlich Opfer ihrer eigenen Popularität, bei beiden wurde das Gesamtwerk von einer einzelnen Sparte überschattet. Schon 1947, ein Jahr nach dem Tod der Künstlerin, formulierte Else Brauneis, damals Professorin an der Akademie der bildenden Künste in München, den Gedanken einer »anderen« Berta Hummel. Sie bezog sich dabei auf Aquarellbilder, die sie im selben Jahr in einer Gedächtnisausstellung in Massing gesehen hatte.[3] Es sollte aber längere Zeit dauern, bis eine Sichtung der Werke Berta Hummels etwa 400 Gemälde und graphische Arbeiten ans Licht brachte, die im kurzen Zeitraum von 1927 bis 1931, das heißt während ihrer Studienjahre in München und vor ihrem Eintritt ins Kloster, entstanden waren. Bei der Vielfalt und erstaunlichen technischen Sicherheit dieser Arbeiten dürfte die einseitige Vorstellung, die die Vermarktung der »Hummelkinder« hat aufkommen lassen, eine Korrektur erfahren.

Berta Hummel wurde am 21. Mai 1909 geboren. Die angesehene Kaufmannsfamilie der Hummels, ursprünglich aus dem Württembergischen stammend, war seit dem 19. Jahrhundert in Massing ansässig, damals ein gemächlicher Marktflecken ländlichen Charakters. Berta wuchs als drittältestes von sieben Kindern in der Geborgenheit eines harmonischen, von religiösen Grundsätzen geprägten Familienlebens auf. Die künstlerische Begabung, die sich schon während ihrer Schuljahre zeigte, wurde besonders von ihrem Vater Adolf Hummel gefördert. Berta blieb ihr Leben lang dankbar für diese Unterstützung und die Ermöglichung eines Kunststudiums in München – etwas, das zu dieser Zeit für ein junges Mädchen vom Land nicht selbstverständlich war. So schrieb sie in einem ihrer ersten Briefe als Studienanfängerin an der Kunstgewerbeschule: »Meinen herzlichen Dank möchte ich Dir [...] aussprechen, für alles was Du mir schon Gutes getan hast. Könnte ich nur das durch Fleiß wieder hereinbringen, was Du schon für mich ausgegeben hast«.[4] Noch die späteren Briefe aus dem Kloster Sießen tragen die Unterzeichnung »Euer dankbares Kind Bertl«.

Hummel child Ady/Hummelkind Ady
1923/25, watercolor, ink/Wasserfarbe, Tinte,
2 $^1/_2$ × 1 $^3/_4$ in./64 × 45 mm
HM 442

Studium in München 1927–1931

Im Sommersemester 1927 nahm Berta Hummel ihr Studium an der Staatlichen Kunstgewerbeschule in München auf. Im Gegensatz zu vielen anderen Städten Deutschlands wurden zu dieser Zeit in München »freie« und »angewandte« Kunst an getrennten Instituten gelehrt.[5] Die
Ausbildung der freien Künstler erfolgte an der Akademie der bildenden Künste, während Stu-
dierende für das staatliche Lehramt die seit 1868 zur Staatsanstalt erhobene Kunstgewerbeschule in der Luisenstraße 37 besuchten. Zur Feier ihres 60-jährigen Bestehens wurde die Staatliche Kunstgewerbeschule im Jahre 1928 in »Staatsschule für angewandte Kunst« umbenannt.
Ein weiterer Namenswechsel zur »Akademie für angewandte Kunst« erfolgte 1937. Nach dem
Krieg wurden dann die beiden Münchener Akademien zur »Hochschule der bildenden Künste«,
später »Akademie der bildenden Künste«, zusammengeschlossen. Nicht uninteressant ist die
Tatsache, dass bis 1919 Frauen vom Studium an der Akademie ausgeschlossen blieben, die
Kunstgewerbeschule aber schon 1872 eine Abteilung eingerichtet hatte, die für die »Heranbil-
dung von Zeichnen-Lehrerinnen« verantwortlich war.[6] Im Lehrplan wurden angeboten: »Line-
arzeichnen mit den nöthigsten Erläuterungen aus der Geometrie, Ornamentenzeichnen, Figurenzeichnen, Blumenzeichnen, Holzschneidekunst, Kunstgeschichte, Perspektive und Schattenlehre.«

Noch als Berta studierte, bestimmte dieser Kanon weitgehend den Studiengang: Ihre erhaltenen Semester- und Prüfungszeugnisse ergeben eine Fächeraufzählung, die fast identisch mit
dem erwähnten Lehrplan aus dem 19. Jahrhundert ist.[7] Die Verpflichtung gegenüber traditionellen Werten bestätigt ebenfalls der Inhalt einer kunstgeschichtlichen Vorlesung, die Berta im
Wintersemester 1930 bei Dr. Hans Kiener besuchte. Durch einen glücklichen Zufall sind ihre
Notizen dazu teilweise erhalten geblieben und bieten einen aufschlussreichen Einblick in den
Lehrstoff. Auch die Professoren Friedrich Wirnhier (1868–1952), Maximilian Dasio (1865–1954)
und Else Brauneis (1877–1959), die Bertas praktisches Kunststudium betreuten, pflegten als
ausübende Künstler eher konservative Stilrichtungen. An den Ausstellungen der Münchener
Künstlergenossenschaft in den Jahren 1929 bis 1933 nahmen sie regelmäßig teil. Noch bis 1937
war Wirnhier mit Gemälden und Zeichnungen in den Katalogen der Großen Münchener Kunst-
ausstellung bzw. der Münchener Jahresausstellung in der Neuen Pinakothek vertreten.

Die Studienjahre in München waren vielleicht die glücklichsten im kurzen Leben der Berta
Hummel. Mit spürbarer Begeisterung schilderte sie in Briefen an Familie und Freunde Alltags-
erlebnisse an der Kunstschule, mit Stolz berichtete sie von persönlichen Erfolgen. Die Eigen-
schaft, ihre einmal gefassten guten Willensentschlüsse mit großer Energie in die Tat umzusetzen, die ihr schon als Kind im Schulzeugnis bescheinigt wurde, entwickelte sich in der anregen-
den Atmosphäre des Studentenlebens zu unermüdlichem Arbeitseifer. Über jede neue Errun-
genschaft freute sie sich, jeden Fortschritt begriff sie als weiterführende Möglichkeit. So erkannte sie im Erlernen von Reproduktionstechniken wie Holzschnitt und Lithographie eine Chance,
eigene Zeichnungen zu vervielfältigen:[8] Schon ab dem ersten Studienjahr ließ sie Holzschnitte
mit verschiedenen Motiven drucken, die sie als Post- und Grußkarten verwandte.

Wenn auch Berta nach eigener Aussage manchmal das Gefühl hatte, sie »stecke ja noch halb
in den Kinderschuhen«,[9] ging sie bei allem, was ihr Werk anbelangte, überraschend sicher und
selbstbewusst vor. Vorzeitig verließ sie die Klasse von Friedrich Wirnhier und schrieb sich in die
höhere Abteilung ein, um bei Maximilian Dasio zu studieren: »Nun Wirnhier war natürlich sehr
unangenehm überrascht, er konnte es gar nicht glauben, er meinte, ich könnte bei Dasio auch
nicht mehr sehen, da ich auch dort zu den Allerbesten gehöre. Kurz u. gut es kränkte fast ein
wenig, daß jetzt seine Allerbeste ging, sagte der Professor, aber es mußte doch mal so kommen. Mir tut es natürlich fürchterlich leid, aber ich kann nichts ändern, ich muß auf meinen
Vorteil bedacht sein. Die Aquarelle soll ich aber Wirnhier noch immer zur Korrektur bringen,
das würde ihn noch freuen, sagte er, das tue ich auch natürlich.«[10] An anderer Stelle heißt es:
»Wirnhier ist stolz, daß er mein Talent entdeckt hat, das meint er nämlich u. ich lasse ihm die
Freude, ich hätte weitaus die beste Mappe.«[11]

Neben seiner vielseitigen künstlerischen Tätigkeit als Medailleur, Maler und Graphiker war
Dasio ein engagierter Lehrer. Seit 1901 wirkte er an der Kunstgewerbeschule und war ab 1920

Ministerialrat im Bayerischen Staatsministerium für Unterricht und Kultus. Auch nach seinem offiziellen Eintritt in den Ruhestand im April 1930 behielt er bis Oktober 1931 die Leitung einer Klasse für Lehramtskandidaten. Außer Else Brauneis ist Dasio der Lehrer, den Berta am häufigsten erwähnte. Sie porträtierte ihn darüber hinaus in zwei Zeichnungen, zwei Aquarellen und einem Holzschnitt (KS M, KS N, KS O, HM 157, HM 636): »Heute besuchte ich Herrn Dasio im Atelier u. denkt Euch, er saß mir wirklich Modell, mit der Zigarre im Mund Zeitung lesend und gelang mir tatsächlich ganz gut, so daß er sehr zufrieden damit war u. die Brauneis steigerte ihr Lob bis zum höchsten Maße, es wäre das Beste das ich machte. ›Wann's wieder Lust hom kommans nur wieder, bin allwei do,‹ sagte mir noch Herr Dasio u. werde es auch ausnützen; denn das ist doch kein Schaden u. auch eine Ehre.«[12] Die Steigerung ins Karikaturhafte bei der Holzschnittvariante dieses Porträts (HM 636) dürfte den leicht skurrilen Humor des Professors besonders angesprochen haben – schon 1920 hatte ihm sein jüngerer Kollege Anton Marxmüller (1898–1984) eine köstliche Folge von Dasio-Karikaturen zum 55. Geburtstag überreicht.[13]

Um die gleiche Zeit wie die Dasio-Porträts entstanden zwei Bildnisse – eine Graphitzeichnung und eine einfühlsame Aquarelldarstellung in Nahsicht – von Else Brauneis, der Professorin, die Berta an der Staatsschule am nächsten stand (KS L, HM 142a). Else Brauneis unterrichtete Aquarelltechnik und die traditionellen Fächer darstellende Geometrie, Perspektive und Schattenlehre. Sie betreute das Seminar für Zeichenlehrerinnen und hatte auch als Leiterin der Bibliothek die Aufgabe, das Interesse der Studenten anzuregen an »den verschiedensten Gebieten durch wechselndes Auflegen von Werken / Ausstellung von Abbildungsmaterial über Einzelgebiete in Zusammenhang mit dem Unterricht in den verschiedenen Klassen«.[14] In der evangelischen Professorin fand Berta Hummel eine strenge, aber zugleich verständnisvolle Mentorin, die einen hohen Arbeitsethos vertrat, der sich nach dem Krieg auf bezeichnende Weise zeigen sollte: Trotz Krankheit und schwieriger Lebensumstände unternahm sie noch mit 70 Jahren den zweistündigen Weg zu Fuß und mit dem Zug zu ihrer Arbeitsstelle, weil sie »am Aufbau unserer alten Akademie rege mitarbeiten« wollte.[15] Else Brauneis war sehr um den beruflichen Erfolg ihrer Studenten besorgt. So war sie bereit, Berta Hummel auch nach dem Klostereintritt durch Beratung und praktische Hilfe tatkräftig zu unterstützen. Vom Abschiedsbesuch bei der Professorin berichtete Berta: »Ich war lange bei ihr – sie ist ein edler Mensch, vor dem man Achtung haben muß. Die Studienfahrten möchte sie so einrichten, daß ich es mir möglich machen kann auch mit zu kommen. Eine Lehrerin wie die Brauneis hatte ich noch nie; und da wurde es mir schon schwer, auch Abschied nehmen zu müssen, um ganz von München zu gehen. [...] Es ist mir schon ein Opfer; aber gerade Sießen hat für mich ein schönes Wirkungsfeld, kann dort künstlerisch und auch in der Schule tätig sein; das schätzt Frau Prof. Brauneis und Paramente ist eines der schönsten Gebiete und darin kann sie mir viel helfen.«[16]

Als Berta bereits im Kloster Sießen lebte, kümmerte sich Else Brauneis um die Überweisung eines Geldbetrags vom Verkauf einer Zeichnung und eines Aquarells und wiederholte ihr Hilfsangebot: »Sind Sie befriedigt von Ihrer Arbeit und arbeiten Sie auch manchmal frei künstlerisch? Nicht liegen lassen Bertl bitte und wenn Sie wollen, Ihre Arbeiten ab und zu schicken.«[17] Es folgt eine Bemerkung über mangelnde Kollegialität unter den Professoren, die ein Licht auf die zunehmend unbehagliche Situation an der Staatsschule wirft: »[...] wir leben ja alle nur nebeneinander hier und nie miteinander. Manchmal friert man bei uns.« Mit dem Aufstieg des nationalsozialistisch gesinnten Professors Richard Klein zum Direktor spitzten sich die Konflikte zu. Der Graphiker Professor Fritz Helmuth Ehmcke, dessen Schriftkurs Berta im Nebenfach besucht hatte, wurde von Klein denunziert – unter anderem, weil er »überhaupt keine Beziehung zum Nationalsozialismus« habe – und verlor seine Stelle.[18] Else Brauneis schilderte auch in einem späteren Brief an Berta Hummel die Verkoppelung von äußerlichen Schwierigkeiten und persönlichem Misstrauen bei Ausbruch des Kriegs: »An unserer Schule sind viele Räume durch Einrichtung einer Rettungsstation verloren gegangen – das ist der Krieg. [...] Da unser Direktor aber Repräsentationsräume braucht, da auch sein Bruder, der aber keine Rechte an unserer Schule hat, auch einen eigenen großen Raum inne hat usw. so erklärte mir Herr Direktor er habe keinen Platz für die Aquarellklasse, und ich ergänzte den Satz ›und gar kein Interesse dafür.‹ Es ist mir sehr leid – denn es waren viele Anfragen da und im Grunde genommen hat Prof. Klein gar keine Ahnung von meiner eigenen Arbeit – auch von dem was es bedeutet von jungen Menschen, die immer nur gelegentlich Zeit für die Aquarellklasse finden, *dennoch* etwas herauszubringen. [...] Schade – aber große Erfolge wie sie Klein hat – steigern nicht immer den Menschen. Jedenfalls ist momentan die Aquarellklasse ›Volk ohne Raum‹ und ohne guten Willen den Raum zu schaffen.«[19]

Berta Hummel dürfte bei ihrem zweiten Aufenthalt in München in den Jahren 1935–1937 am neuen Geist in der Staatsschule sehr gelitten haben. Während ihrer ersten Studienzeit dort blieb sie jedoch von allen Anzeichen kommenden Unheils unbehelligt. Sie beobachtete zwar, dass »Dasio nicht mehr sehr viel zu sagen hat, dafür Prof. Klein, ein sehr bedeutender Künstler«. Die Benotung sei deshalb allgemein härter geworden, aber »Prof. Klein sagte aus, daß eine einzige wirklich künstlerisch begabt sei u. wirklich viel könne, u. die sei vom Rottal, mit der könne er was anfangen, meinte er. Wieder ein Prof. der mich gern wollte«.[20] Und ein paar Tage später: »[...] von allen Seiten werde ich bestürmt, jeder Prof. würde es sich für eine Freude und Ehre schätzen, mich in die künstlerische Laufbahn weiterzuführen (Prof. Klein, Prof. Jaskolla – Brauneis, Pretorius – Kornmann, Prof. Kolb).«[21] Auf die alte Rivalität zwischen den Instituten freier und angewandter Kunst anspielend, erwähnt der gleiche Brief eine geplante Ausstellung an der Staatsschule: »Durch die Ausstellung soll eben gezeigt werden, daß auch Zeichenlehrerinnen künstlerisches leisten können.«

Das Werk

Die Unbeschwertheit und innere Ausgeglichenheit Berta Hummels in diesen ersten Münchener Jahren spiegeln sich in einem produktiven, vielseitigen Schaffen wider, das Landschaften, Stadtansichten, Blumenstudien, Stillleben, Porträts, Kinderbilder, Karikaturen und Dekorationsarbeiten umfasst. Ebenso divers sind die Techniken: Holzschnitt und Lithographie, Zeichnungen in Bleistift, Graphit, Rötel und Kohle, Gemälde in Aquarell und Öl.

Ab 1928 wandte sie sich immer mehr dem Aquarell zu, das ihrer lockeren, raschen Malweise und sicheren Farbempfindung entgegenkam. In dieser Technik erreichte sie ihre größte künstlerische Freiheit. Bilder wie »Mädchen in Tracht« (HM 196a) oder die Kopfstudie ihres Hundes »Lord« (HM 210) geraten zu reinen Farbstudien: Ersteres ein übermütiges Spiel mit flüchtig nebeneinandergesetzten, kräftig kontrastierenden Streifen, aus denen ein Körper entsteht, letzteres eine fast monochrome Harmonie mit zartesten Nuancen. Die straffe Rhythmik in »Über den Dächern« (HM 352) steht wiederum im Dienst einer abstrahierenden Geometrie. Aus der Vogelperspektive ergeben Straßenzüge und Häuserdächer ein komplexes Gefüge übergreifender Diagonalen. Die gleiche Annäherung an ein abstraktes Prinzip bestimmt die bewusste Strukturierung einer Marktszene (HM 265) durch eine stufenartige Anordnung in Horizontalreihen, die sich formal wie farblich klar voneinander absetzen. In Kompositionen dieser Art wird »der Bildgegenstand unbedeutend: er verschwindet gleichsam im Bild, das als in sich ruhendes Form- und Farbgefüge sich selbst genügt.«[22] Ein scheinbar zufälliger Ausschnitt, der Blick aus einem unerwarteten Winkel reicht aus, um die Vorstellung eines ganzen Objekts, etwa eines alten ärmlichen Hauses (HM 206), heraufzubeschwören.

Anders als bei ihren wenigen Ölbildern aus der Studienzeit, die alle bei einer fast abbildartigen Wiedergabe verharren, zeigte sich Berta beim Aquarell experimentierfreudig und erprobte mit offensichtlichem Interesse die vielfältigen Möglichkeiten der Technik. Sie arbeitete hauptsächlich Nass in Nass. Der weiße Papiergrund wird zum hellsten Wert, indem er beim Farbauftrag ausgespart bleibt. Der Gewinn an Leuchtkraft in den Arbeiten aus den Jahren 1928-1930 kommt besonders den Blumenbildern zugute. Virtuos ist das Zusammenspiel von Bildidee und Technik in der Studie »Dame in Rot« (HM 239). Die schlanke, schöne Gestalt im schlichten roten Kleid strahlt eine unmittelbare Präsenz aus – obwohl sie sich vom Betrachter abwendet, nachsinnend über etwas, das der Außenwelt verborgen bleibt. Der Eindruck des Geheimnisvollen und Unerreichbaren, den die Haltung der Figur evoziert, wird von der Flüchtigkeit und der lichten Transparenz des Farbauftrags unterstrichen. Eine zunehmende Entfernung vom Gegenständlichen zeigt sich mal in der Auflösung in flächige Farbpartien, wie bei dem Portrait der Else Brauneis (HM 142a) oder der stillen, altarähnlichen Innenraumszene (HM 868), mal in hastigen, frei eingesetzten Pinselstrichen, etwa bei der Studie eines Bauern (HM 938a) oder der heiteren Dampferpartie auf dem Chiemsee (HM 869).

Es ist zu bedauern, dass Berta Hummel nach ihrem Klostereintritt die Aquarellmalerei zugunsten des Pastells mehr oder weniger aufgab. Einige wenige Blumenbilder, die nachweislich in ihren späteren Sießener Jahren entstanden, wurden weitgehend in »stehender Farbe« ausgeführt. Ihnen fehlen die Transparenz und die Spontaneität der Arbeiten in reiner Aquarelltechnik.

Mit fast 80 Bildern sind die Blumenstudien die zweitgrößte Werkgruppe der »anderen« Berta Hummel. Von den frühen Semestern 1927/28 stammen sensible Bleistiftzeichnungen, die in ihrer Genauigkeit der botanischen Illustration ähneln: Das Pflanzenleben wird oft in verschiedenen Stadien von der Knospe über die Blüte bis zum Verwelken erfasst (HM 179-191, KS A-C). Die aus präziser Beobachtung resultierenden Erfahrungen werden in den Blumenaquarellen der Jahre 1928–1930 frei umgesetzt: Diese Bilder leben von der Farbe. Kräftige Kontraste setzen Akzente in den farbprächtigen Kompositionen HM 221b und HM 523. Einen Gegensatz dazu bilden die zurückhaltenden Töne der Chrysantheme (HM 333) oder die flüchtigen, zart gesetzten Striche in HM 311, die die zerbrechliche Schönheit und Vergänglichkeit des Blumenlebens heraufbeschwören.

Beim Vergleich zwischen den sorgfältigen Bleistiftzeichnungen, die noch nahe am Modell bleiben, und der offenen Entfaltung in den Aquarellen erscheint eine spätere Aussage der Künstlerin relevant. Während ihres zweiten Studiums in München beantwortete Maria Innocentia Fragen ihres Bruders Franz über das Malen. Ein Brief vom 09.06.1936 enthält in nuce ihr künstlerisches Credo: »Nimm ein kleines Blümchen, einen Grashalm, sieh es Dir genau an, vergleiche wie verschieden u. mannigfaltig ihre Gestaltung ist, dann gehe heim u. zeichne was Du beobachtet u. gesehen hast, Du wirst sehen, wie notwendig es ist, erst richtig zu ›schauen‹ lernen, dann aber wie wichtig es ist das Wesen zu erfassen. Nehme an, das hilflose, schwankende des Grashalms, das stärrige u. stachelige des Gesträpps, das ›stillblühen‹ des Veilchens – oder besser aus der Tierwelt – das Wesen des Adlers von dem einer Taube. [...] Nicht das ist das Wichtigste, daß Du richtig u. genau abzeichnest; sondern daß Du das Wesen des Dinges erfasst, Dich hineinlebst u. dann auszudrücken suchst. [...] Du sollst Nutzen daraus ziehen, nicht Unverständnis u. Unwahrhaftigkeit, denn wenn man etwas macht, was man nicht versteht, ist es nicht wahr. [...] Gewöhne Dir an, ehrlich zu sein u. nichts dem Zufall zu überlassen, jeden Strich bewusst zu machen. Wie in der Natur nichts ohne Beziehung ist, so muss jeder Strich zum Ganzen eine Beziehung haben; z. Bsp. ein Baum, Stamm, Äste, Zweige, Blätter beziehen sich aufeinander, eines geht aus dem Andern hervor. Du musst Dir angewöhnen richtig zu zeichnen, wie es das Wachstum Dich lehrt – also nicht das Nebensächliche, bevor die Hauptsache da ist – nicht zuerst die Augen, die Nase u. die Glanzlichter darauf, bevor der Kopf da ist – nicht zuerst die Federn, bevor der Vogel da ist. Das sind die größten Anfängerfehler, die meisten legen sie nie ab, zum Teil weil man es ihnen nicht lehrte, oder weil sie es nicht können aus Mangel an Ausdauer.«

Die Landschaften und Stadtansichten von Berta Hummel gehören ausnahmslos in die Münchener Studienzeit. Die große Mehrheit entstand 1928–1930, vereinzelte Beispiele folgten beim zweiten Studienaufenthalt 1935/36. Berta beschäftigte sich gern mit dieser Thematik. Später, nach dem Eintritt ins Kloster, bedauerte sie, dass sie keine Möglichkeit mehr dazu fand: »Manchmal juckt mich schon die Lust, wie ehedem in den Gäßchen u. Winkeln zu malen, was als Schwester nicht gut geht«.[23] Die Bandbreite ihrer Darstellungen verdeutlichen schon die vier erhaltenen Aquarellansichten von München, die die vielgesichtigen Reize der Großstadt zeigen: kleinteilige, fast nervöse Detailarbeit beim Blick über das Gewirr der Dächer (HM 852), strenge, strukturelle Reduzierung bei HM 265, ein bunter Komplex verwinkelter Häuser im volkstümlichen Au-Viertel (HM 863a) und ein in einheitlicher Farbgebung gehaltener und dadurch großräumig wirkender Anblick der repräsentativen »Ludwigstraße« (HM 942). Auch von Salzburg sind mehrere Ansichten erhalten, die während Studienexkursionen gemalt wurden. Briefe von Else Brauneis erwähnen Ausflüge nach Lindau und Salzburg, wo Berta oben in der Festung wohnte. In zeitlicher Nähe da-

Hummel child Franz/Hummelkind Franz
1923/25, watercolor, ink/Wasserfarbe, Tinte,
2 $^3/_4$ × 2 in./68 × 53 mm
HM 443

zu stehen Gebirgslandschaften aus dem Salzburger Land und der Chiemsee-Gegend. Eine weitere, farbintensive Bildgruppe hat Wald- und Baumstudien zum Thema.

Einen wichtigen Platz nehmen die Darstellungen aus Bertas Geburtsort Massing ein. Die tiefe Verbundenheit mit ihrer Heimat, die sich immer wieder in ihrem Werk spiegelt, wurde in ihrer Kindheit manifestiert. Damals waren es die Ausflüge zum Malen zusammen mit ihrem Vater und ihrer Schwester Centa (Kreszentia), die ihr Interesse anregten und ihr Empfinden für den spezifischen Charakter der Rottaler Gegend schärften. Später nahm sie in den Semesterferien, die sie zu Hause verbrachte, das Altvertraute mit neuen Augen wahr. Den Auftakt der circa 50 Ansichten aus Massing und der Umgebung bildet eine Gruppe von Holzschnitten und Tuschezeichnungen, darunter eine charmant-verspielte Marktszene mit Bertas Geburtshaus als Kulisse (HM 623). Bemerkenswerte Kunstfertigkeit zeigt sich beim Kontrast zwischen dem hellen, großflächigen Hintergrund und der dunkel gehaltenen, bewegten Szene mit fast tänzerisch wirkenden kleinen Figuren im Vordergrund. Hier treten Motive auf, die später zum Repertoire der typischen »Hummelbilder« wurden und noch bei den allerletzten Arbeiten, den als »Letztes Schenken« posthum herausgegebenen Zeichnungen, zu finden sind, beispielsweise das tratschende Bauernvolk mit übergroßen Füssen und riesigen Regenschirmen. Das Hummelhaus steht am östlichen Ende des Marktplatzes. Von hier aus konnte Berta das geschäftige Treiben an den Buden beobachten (HM 486, HM 46). Sie kannte den sonst belebten Platz aber auch als Ort weihnachtlicher Stille (HM 618) und in der Ruhe des frühen Morgens: Wie in einem Traumbild verharrt ein Pferd geduldig vor seinem Fuhrwerk auf dem noch menschenleeren Platz (HM 651). Die gleiche Atmosphäre träumerischer Ruhe bestimmt den Blick, am Hummelhaus vorbei, in die Zufahrtsstraße zum Markt – jetzt die Berta-Hummel-Straße – mit ausgreifenden, amorphen Schattenpartien, die einen Gegensatz zu den geraden Linien der Häuserzeile bilden (HM 652). Da viele der alten Handwerkerhäuser von damals längst abgerissen wurden und ganze Straßenzüge sich heute mit einem anderen Erscheinungsbild präsentieren, haben Bertas Ansichten, über ihre künstlerische Aussage hinausgehend, eine besondere Signifikanz als Dokumente der Ortsgeschichte, zumal eine beträchtliche Anzahl der Darstellungen von Massing und dem Umland genaue Datierungsvermerke tragen. Berta Hummel schilderte auch das lokale Leben und Brauchtum: die »Fronleichnamsprozession« (HM 498) oder den Rundgang des Nachtwächters (HM 649), das zänkische Handeln beim »Viehmarkt« (HM 858A) ebenso wie die stille Arbeit des Schusters in seiner Werkstube (HM 644, HM 645).

Wie sehr Berta in ihrem Heimatort verwurzelt war, äußert sich auf besondere Art in der Auswahl des Themas »Massing« für das Geschenk zur Silberhochzeit ihrer Eltern, einen großen Wandbehang in Applikationstechnik. Hier setzte sie Massinger Wahrzeichen und Motive aus dem bäuerlichen Leben collagenartig zusammen – nicht als reelle Stadtansicht, sondern gleichsam als ideelle »Summa« ihrer bisherigen Welt, vor dem Aufbruch zu einem neuen Leben im Kloster Sießen (HM 493B).

Berta's sisters at the piano/Katharina und Viki am Klavier
1926, pencil/Bleistift, 5 $^3/_4$ × 6 $^1/_2$ in./145 × 165 mm
HM 45

Die Eindrücke und Erlebnisse der frühen Jahre ließen sie nie los. In den im Kloster entstandenen Bildern mit den beliebten Kindersujets kehrt ein auf Erinnerungen zurückgehender Motivschatz immer wieder. Bestimmte Objekte tauchen in stilisierter Form auf und werden wie Theaterrequisiten in den Kontext der Darstellungen eingefügt: der Lattenzaun, der in vielen Massinger Ansichten zu sehen ist, die Tanne, das Marterl am Feldweg, das ruhige Flusstal und die sanften Hügel der Rottaler Landschaft. Die »Hummelbilder«, so klischeehaft sie bisweilen erscheinen, konnten nur auf der Grundlage erlebter Wirklichkeit entstehen.

Am Beginn der Reihe der Porträts stehen mehrere Bildnisse von Bertas Familie und der weiteren Verwandtschaft. Darstellungen von Bekannten, Studien aus dem Bauernleben und Arbeiten mit den Modellen der Staatsschule kommen dazu. Zwei Selbstporträts verraten, wie Berta sich selbst in diesen Jahren sah. Das erste, eine Bleistiftzeichnung aus dem Jahr 1928 (HM 432), wird vom wachen, kritischen Blick der 19jährigen beherrscht. Die Augen sind immer noch die dominante Partie des Gesichts im zweiten, ein Jahr später entstandenen Porträt in Rötel (HM 514), der Ausdruck hier ist aber zurückhaltender, fast verletzlich. Die umfangreiche Gruppe der Porträts bezeugt die Offenheit, mit der die junge Berta Hummel ihrer Umwelt begegnete. Allen, ob Bekannten oder professionellen Modellen, brachte sie die gleiche Anteilnahme entgegen im Bestreben, über die rein protokollarische Aufnahme physiognomischer Eigenarten hinausgehend den Dargestellten in seiner Ganzheit zu erfassen.

Gleich bei der Aufnahmeprüfung für die Staatsschule sah sie sich mit einem Thema konfrontiert, das zum Großstadtalltag der späten 20er Jahre gehörte, für Berta aber, an das behütete Leben in einer gutsituierten Kleinstadtfamilie

The conductor/Dirigent im Frack
1926.07, pencil/Bleistift, 9 $^1/_4$ × 12 $^3/_4$ in./238 × 321 mm
HM 567

gewöhnt, neu und fremd gewesen sein muss. Sie berichtete in einem Brief vom 12.6.1927, sie habe »einen ganz ausgehungerten Mann zeichnen« müssen.[24] Wenn auch die kunsttechnische Aufgabenstellung hier das Herausarbeiten der Knochenstruktur beinhaltete, lag zugleich eine bedrückende Aktualität in der Sujetauswahl: Man musste nach derartigen Zeugnissen der damaligen Armut nicht weit suchen, wie sie beispielsweise in den Bildern von Käthe Kollwitz mit erschütternder Eindringlichkeit vor Augen geführt wurden.

Technisch sind die Porträts die vielfältigste Werkgruppe Berta Hummels. Sie arbeitete in Tusche, Bleistift, Rötel und Pastell, später vorwiegend in Aquarell und Kohle. Die Aquarelle umfassen so verschiedene Bilder wie die elegante Kostümstudie der »Dame in Blau« (HM 243), die auffallenden Charakterköpfe HM 149a und HM 156 und einige Kinderporträts (HM 128, HM 214, HM 238). Letztere sind Bildnisse im eigentlichen Sinn, weit entfernt von der schematischen Verniedlichung der »Hummelkinder«. Der kleine Junge, der still und selbstvergessen ein Bilderbuch betrachtet (HM 50), oder das unsicher zur Seite blickende Mädchen (HM 236) werden mit der gleichen Einsicht und Ernsthaftigkeit beobachtet wie die erwachsenen Modelle. Ihre größte Ausdrucksstärke beim Porträt erreichte Berta aber in den Kohlezeichnungen. Ihre Kenntnis expressionistischer Porträtkunst zeigen die Darstellungen der alten Margret, die ihre Hässlichkeit als Malmodell an der Staatsschule zur Schau stellte. Berta, offensichtlich von dieser bizarren Erscheinung fasziniert, porträtierte sie mehrmals: das lange, knochige Gesicht mit hochgezogenen Brauen und eingefallenen Wangen, die müden, glanzlosen Augen, den fast zahnlosen Mund mit wulstiger Unterlippe (HM 147, HM 148, HM 200, KS P, KS Q, KS R). Bemerkenswert ist, dass die eindringlichsten Porträts der Künstlerin, die durch die heiteren »Hummelkinder« bekannt wurde, das Alter thematisieren. Mit tiefem Mitgefühl und dennoch ohne falschen Pathos registrierte sie die Desillusion und Resignation des alten Menschen, die Hinfälligkeit eines ausgezehrten, schon vom Tode gezeichneten Greises (HM 229), aber auch die stille Würde einer alten Bäuerin beim Lesen in ihrem Gebetbuch (HM 198).

Von Berta Hummels Karikaturen sind heute nur wenige erhalten. Sie dürfte in der Studienzeit viel mehr geschaffen haben, denn nach Notizen von Schwester Maria Laura Brugger, ihrer Mitstudentin an der Staatsschule und der späteren Betreuerin des im Kloster Sießen erhaltenen Teils ihres künstlerischen Nachlasses, »pflegte sie die charakteristische Erscheinung des Professors Dasio in verschiedenen Karikaturen festzuhalten.«[25] So fiel gleich auf Berta Verdacht, als eine derartige Darstellung zufällig in einem Papierkorb entdeckt wurde: »Frau Professor Else Brauneis erkannte sofort den genialen Entwurf [...] und sagte lächelnd: ›Das kann nur eine sein: das Lausmädel in der Dasio-Klasse.‹ Dasio selbst erhielt auch Kenntnis davon und sagte ohne jegliche Spur von Empfindlichkeit: ›Sagen Sie dem Lausmädel, sie hätte ruhig die Schublade weiter herausziehen dürfen.‹ (Mit Schublade meinte er seine gewohnheitsmäßig weit vorgeschobene Unterlippe).«[26] Zwei Grußkarten zum Neujahr 1930 (HM 65, HM 846) wurden in der ersten Auflage des »Hummel-Buchs« von 1934 publiziert. Aus der

»Betrunkenen Perspektive« (HM 846) geraten die fein gezeichneten Stufengänge und hohen Häuser der Großstadt ins Wanken. Selbst die Initialen der Künstlerin, »B.H.«, verdrehen sich zum Signum »HB« auf einem Hofbräuhaus-Maßkrug. Berta machte sich auch über das Bauernvolk lustig (HM 192, HM 193). Die Gruppe dreier Klatschbasen ist in scharf differenzierter Typisierung gezeichnet: die Überrundliche (mit passend ausbauschendem Regenschirm), die Bebrillte, emsig Neuigkeiten kolportierend, und die boshafte Dürre mit verkniffenem Mund und spitzem Kinn, eine Vorgängerin späterer Hexentypen. Ebenso erschreckend sind ihrerseits die Männer, die wie Personifikationen von Dummheit, Verschlagenheit und Selbstgefälligkeit auftreten. Die gleichen Personen feilschen zankend am »Viehmarkt« und reihen sich heuchlerisch frömmelnd in die »Fronleichnamsprozession« ein (HM 885A, HM 886). In der Übersteigerung der Komik bei einer Rauferei zwischen zwei kleinen Buben (HM 64) lieferte Berta einen Prototyp für die späteren »Hummelkinder«. Einige der gelungensten »Hummelkind«-Darstellungen stehen in der Tat der Karikatur nahe: etwa die präzis geschilderten Situationen bei der Serie der »Berufe«, in der Kinder – mit mehr oder weniger Erfolg – die Beschäftigungen der Erwachsenenwelt nachahmen, oder das Bildpaar mit »Maler« und »Kunstkritiker«, wo humorvoll die Quintessenz aus Erfahrungen im eigenen Arbeitsbereich herausgearbeitet wird.

Aus der Anfangszeit an der Staatsschule sind Arbeiten erhalten, die zur angewandten Kunst im eigentlichen Sinn gehören, darunter Entwürfe für eine Kindertapete (HM 16-19) und einen Fäustling (HM 469). Für eine nicht näher spezifizierte »Studie« für die Firma Stabilo erhielt Berta im ersten Studienjahr eine Anzahlung.[27] Auch Lebzelterentwürfe gehörten zum Handwerk: Bekanntlich fertigte Maximilian Dasio 1898/99 Lebzelterentwürfe für die Firma Ebenböck an.[28] Bertas Lebzelterentwurf zeigt »Hänsel und Gretel bei der Hexe« (KS). Für das Geschäft ihrer Familie schuf sie 1929 aufwendige Schaufensterdekorationen zu Ostern und Weihnachten (HM 453, HM 448) und ein Firmenzeichen mit stilisierter Hummel. Das Wortspiel mit ihrem Familiennamen amüsierte sie stets. Als junges Mädchen »porträtierte« sie sich und ihre Geschwister in einer köstlichen Folge miniaturhafter »Charakterstudien« als Hummeln, und noch in ihr Spätwerk fügte sie das Motiv einer heranfliegenden Hummel als eine Art piktographische Signatur ein.

Entscheidung für das Kloster

Der Eintritt der erst 22jährigen Berta Hummel in das Franziskanerinnenkloster Sießen am 22. April 1931 hatte eine thematische, technische und stilistische Verlagerung in ihrem Schaffen zur Folge.

Ihre bisherige Motivwahl musste den vom Kloster gestellten Aufgaben weichen. Diese waren vielfach: Arbeit im angesehenen Sießener Paramentensaal (dessen künstlerische Leitung sie 1934 übernahm), Zeichenunterricht in der Schule St. Anna in Saulgau, die Anfertigung von Altargemälden und kleinen Andachtsbildern für die Verlage Ver Sacrum, Rottenburg, Emil Fink Verlag, Stuttgart, Ars sacra sowie die Gesellschaft für christliche Kunst, München und vor allem auch die Entwürfe für die »Hummelkinder«-Karten. Im August 1933 fand die klösterliche Einkleidung statt. Sie erhielt den Klosternamen Maria Innocentia, die Werke ab diesem Zeitpunkt tragen meist die Signatur »M. I. Hummel«. Die Publikation des »Hummel-Buchs« 1934 im Emil Fink Verlag, Stuttgart, steigerte entscheidend die Bekanntheit und Popularität Maria Innocentias. Der kunstinteressierte Bischof von Regensburg, Dr. Michael Buchberger, bemerkte zum Erfolg des Buches, sie habe damit »die Volksseele getroffen.«[29] Zugleich sah Buchberger die latente Gefahr der künstlerischen Einengung voraus: »Sie braucht auch eine große und ernste Aufgabe, um an derselben geistig, seelisch und künstlerisch zu wachsen.«[30] Er lud sie ein, eine geplante Schulbibel zu illustrieren. Ihre zunächst gegebene Zusage musste Maria Innocentia zurücknehmen, weil die Klosterleitung ihre Arbeit am Bibelprojekt untersagte[31] und dem Wunsch der Porzellanmanufaktur Goebel, die »Hummelkinder«-Karten in plastische Form umzusetzen, den Vorzug gab. Nur zögernd stimmte Maria Innocentia zu. Für sie war es zunächst eine Frage des künstlerischen Gewissens, inwieweit ihre Kompositionen die Verwandlung ins Dreidimensionale zuließen, ob der nuancenreiche Linienduktus der Kohlezeichnung ohne Qualitätsverlust in eine rundplastische Gestalt zu übersetzten wäre. Die Hummelfiguren hatten aber trotzdem einen immensen Erfolg. Maria Innocentia fand sich damit den harten Gesetzen der Vermarktung ausgeliefert. Mit der Verpflichtung zur Anfertigung immer neuer Kindermotive verengte sich ihre Thematik: Stadtbild und Landschaft verschwanden, das Blumenbild tauchte nur gelegentlich auf, das Porträt verkümmerte oft zum Schematismus.

Die neuen Tätigkeiten verlangten ihrerseits neue technische Verfahren. Berta hatte sich auf die Arbeit in der Paramentenwerkstatt gefreut, die sie gleich einen Tag nach ihrer Ankunft in Sießen aufnahm. Schon bei dem Wandbehang »Massing« hatte sie die Gelegenheit wahrgenommen, Möglichkeiten der Textilarbeit zu erproben. Auch ihre Erwähnung der Textilspezialistin und Professorin Else Jaskolla als eine der Lehrkräfte, die ihre Arbeit gern weiterbetreut hätten, deutet auf ihre Erfolge in diesem Bereich an der Staatsschule hin.[32] Ein erster Entwurf zu einem Messgewand (HM 565) stammt noch aus der Studienzeit, zwei kleinformatige Madonnendarstellungen (HM 70, HM 71) um die Zeit des Klostereintritts stellen frühe Übungsstücke dar, die ihre Auseinandersetzung mit den spezifischen Flächenproblemen der Paramentik zeigen. Ferner machte sie sich Sorgen über die gedruckte Wiedergabe ihrer Vorlagen bei den Andachtsbildern und Hummelkarten: »[...] es ist für mich sehr wichtig, das Reproduktionsverfahren zu kennen, damit ich beim Arbeiten auf technische Schwierigkeiten Rücksicht nehmen kann.«[33] Im Versuch, den Erfordernissen des Druckwerks von vornherein durch geeignete künstlerische Mittel entgegenzukommen, stellte sie sich auf Pastellarbeiten ein. So sind die große Mehrzahl der für die Reproduktion geschaffenen Kinderbilder als Pastell- und Kohlezeichnungen ausgeführt. Im Falle der Altargemälde waren dagegen Arbeiten in Öl erwünscht. Die Entwürfe dazu wurden in Gouache, Tempera und Mischtechnik geliefert.

Unter den Zwängen der Auftragsarbeit musste Maria Innocentia zur bitteren Erkenntnis kommen, dass es nicht möglich sein würde, ihre Zielsetzungen als Künstlerin mit denjenigen als Ordensfrau in Einklang zu bringen. Die Korrespondenz über das gescheiterte Bibelprojekt ergibt ein trauriges Bild der Niedergeschlagenheit und Selbstzweifel, die Maria Innocentia bei Verhandlungen in München zeigte.[34] Einer Klosterleitung, die mehr Verständnis für ihre Ernsthaftigkeit als Künstlerin aufgebracht hätte, wären die Anzeichen beklemmender innerer Not nicht unverborgen geblieben. Aber Maria Innocentia blieb mit dem Konflikt allein. Sie konnte ihn nur auf ihre Weise sublimieren: mit dem großartigen, 1936 begonnenen Kreuzweg, von dem etwa 50 Entwürfe, zum Teil im Kloster Sießen und zum Teil im Berta-Hummel-Museum in Massing, erhalten sind. Dieser düstere, expressionistische Zyklus ist das persönlichste Werk der Maria Innocentia Hummel aus diesen Jahren, ein letztes Aufflackern eines privaten Kunstwollens ohne Konzessionen an das Wunschbild einer »heilen Welt«. Es ist die folgerichtige Fortsetzung des Weges, den sie in den letzten Kohleporträts der Studienzeit eingeschlagen hatte. Es war Maria Innocentia nicht vergönnt, diesen Weg weiterzugehen. Aus ihrem Verständnis des Ordenslebens heraus entschloss sie sich freiwillig, ihre Arbeit in den Dienst Anderer zu stellen. Ihre letzten Jahre wurden weitgehend von Auftragsarbeiten bestimmt. Erst 37 Jahre alt, starb Schwester Maria Innocentia Hummel am 6. November 1946 an Tuberkulose in Sießen.

Anmerkungen

1 Kurt Flemig, Karikaturisten-Lexikon, München, New Providence u.a. 1993, S. 128.

2 Die Hummelfiguren selbst wurden nicht von M. Innocentia modelliert, sondern nach ihren Vorlagen von Modelleuren der W. Goebel Porzellanfabrik angefertigt.

3 »Ihre Aquarelle wieder zu sehen war mir große Freude und darin steckt die andere damals so fröhliche Bertel Hummel«, Brief von Else Brauneis an Adolf Hummel vom 09.09.47, Berta-Hummel-Museum Massing (BHM Massing).

4 Brief vom 15.06.27.

5 Winfried Nerdinger, Fatale Kontinuität, in: Thomas Zacharias (Hrsg.), Tradition und Widerspruch – 175 Jahre Kunstakademie München, München 1985, S. 54: »Während nach dem Vorbild des Bauhauses in Weimar auch in Berlin, Karlsruhe, Breslau oder Stuttgart Kunstgewerbeschulen und Akademien zusammengelegt wurden, beharrte München auf der strikten Trennung von freier und angewandter Kunst.«

6 Zur Geschichte der Kunstgewerbeschule siehe Wolfgang Kehr, Kunsterzieher an der Akademie, in: Thomas Zacharias (Hrsg.), Tradition und Widerspruch – 175 Jahre Kunstakademie München, München 1985, S. 287ff.

7 Im Zeugnis der »Lehramtsprüfung für Zeichenlehrerinnen«, datiert 18. März 1931, werden folgende Fächer benotet: »Projektionszeichnen, perspektivisches Zeichnen, Ornamentzeichnen, Figurenzeichnen: Kopfmodell nach dem Leben, Figurenzeichnen: Gewandfigur nach dem Leben, Blumenzeichnen nach der Natur, farbige Darstellung nach der Natur, Entwerfen eines Ornaments, Lehrprobe und Methodik des Zeichenunterrichts, Kunstgeschichte, Stillehre.« Der Beleg der Fächer Holzschnitt (bei dem Xylograph Albert Fallscheer), Lithographie (bei Bartholomäus Neumeier), Aquarellieren und darstellende Geometrie (bei Professor Else Brauneis) ist in Semesterzeugnissen dokumentiert.

8 Brief an eine Freundin vom 12.06.27, Fotokopie BHM Massing.

9 Brief von Prof. Else Brauneis vom 26.10.31, BHM Massing.

10 Brief vom 07.10.28, BHM Massing.

11 Brief vom 14.11.31, BHM Massing.

12 Brief vom 15.01.30, BHM Massing.

13 Ingrid S. Weber, Maximilian Dasio 1865 – 1954. Münchner Maler, Medailleur und Ministerialrat. Ausstellungskatalog München 1985, S. 180f.

14 Staatliche Kunstgewerbeschule München. Auszug aus den Bestimmungen und dem Lehrplan (o. J., vermutl. um 1927), S. 15.

15 Brief von Else Brauneis an Adolf Hummel vom 01.05.47.

16 Brief vom 20.03.31, BHM Massing.

17 Brief von Else Brauneis vom 26.10.31: »Ich muss Ihnen herzlichen Gruß senden – und 80 Mark für den Verkauf einer Bleistiftzeichnung Wetterlaune und einem Aquarell Hafen in Lindau. [...] Gekauft hat das Aquarell (50 M) und die Zeichnung (30 M) Direktor Beck von der Rupprechtstraße. Ich traf ihn einmal in ehrlicher Begeisterung in der Aquarellausstellung, die ich von meiner Klasse gemacht hatte und wo Ihre Arbeiten wohl der Glanzpunkt waren.«

18 Thomas Zacharias, (Art) reine Kunst. Die Münchener Akademie um 1937, München 1987, S. 10.

19 Brief vom 11.12.39, BHM Massing.

20 Brief vom 14.03.31, BHM Massing.

21 Brief vom 20.03.31, BHM Massing.

22 Martin Ortmeier, Das andere Werk der Berta Hummel, in: Die andere Berta Hummel. Unbekannte Werke einer bekannten Künstlerin, Ausstellungskatalog der Kunstsammlung des Bistums Regensburg (Kataloge und Schriften Bd. 3), Diözesanmuseum Regensburg, München, Zürich 1986, S. 21.

23 Brief vom 15.07.38, BHM Massing.

24 Brief vom 12.06.27, Kopie im BHM Massing.

25 Schriftliche Mitteilung von Schwester M. Witgard Erler, Kloster Sießen.

26 ebenda.

27 Postkarte vom 18.12.27, BHM Massing.

28 Ingrid S. Weber, a. a. O., S. 20.

29 Brief vom 29.12.34 von Bischof Buchberger an den Verlag Josef Kösel & Friedrich Pustet. Bischöfliches Zentralarchiv, Regensburg.

30 Brief vom 29.12.1934 von Bischof Buchberger an die Familie Hummel, BHM Massing.

31 Vgl. Briefe von Bischof Buchberger an Schwester Innocentia Hummel vom 03.12.34 und an Kloster Sießen vom 12.04.35.

32 Vgl. Brief vom 20.03.31, BHM Massing.

33 Brief vom 22.05.33, BHM Massing.

34 Brief vom 11.07.35 vom Verlag Josef Kösel & Friedrich Pustet an Bischof Buchberger. Bischöfliches Zentralarchiv, Regensburg.

»Hummel Bertl, zeichne mich!«
Centa erinnert sich
an ihre Schwester Berta

Eine besonders enge Beziehung hatte Berta Hummel zu ihrer zwei Jahre jüngeren Schwester Kreszentia, genannt Centa. Neben der gemeinsamen Schulzeit festigten zusammen verbrachte Urlaube und zahlreiche Besuche Centas in München und später im Kloster Sießen die Verbindung der beiden. Centa Hummel, die eine lebendige Erinnerung an diese Zeit hegt, lebt heute in Passau. Das Gespräch führte Claudia Bauer.

Ihr Vater, Adolf Hummel, wollte eigentlich Bildhauer werden und zeigte auch später, nachdem er eine kaufmännische Laufbahn eingeschlagen hatte, starkes kulturelles Engagement. Lag das künstlerische Talent Ihrer Schwester Berta in der Familie?

Eigentlich waren beide Elternteile sehr musisch veranlagte Personen, aber es stimmt schon, dass hauptsächlich der Vater eine besondere künstlerische Ader hatte. Er war der einzige Sohn der Familie, also musste er gegen seinen Wunsch, Bildhauer zu werden, den von seinem Vater Jakob Hummel gegründeten Kolonialwarenhandel in Massing übernehmen. Neben seinem Beruf als Kaufmann war er auch noch Bürgermeister, schrieb die Massinger Ortschronik und erhielt später die Ehrenbürgerwürde. Sein Geschäft hat ihn sehr vereinnahmt, dennoch setzte er sich Abends oft hin und ging seinen »Liebhabereien« nach, so hat er beispielsweise kleine Holzschatullen mit Brandmalereien verziert und sie anschließend seiner Frau geschenkt. Wir Kinder durften ihm bei dieser Arbeit zuschauen und haben das sehr genossen.

Auch auf der Seite der Mutter gab es eine Künstlerin: Ihre Schwester, also unsere Tante, malte Ölbilder. Unsere Mutter war, wie schon erwähnt, ebenfalls nicht untalentiert, hatte aber durch die Mitarbeit im Geschäft und die Familie keine Zeit, wirklich aktiv zu werden.

Von uns Kindern waren alle künstlerisch recht bewandert. Ich hatte ein inniges Verhältnis zu Berta und in den Anfängen unserer gemeinsamen Schulzeit drängte sie mich stets zu einer Ausbildung an der Kunstgewerbeschule. Damals wollte Berta noch Turnlehrerin werden.

Centa and Berta on a swing, 1916/17
Centa und Berta auf der Schaukel, 1916/17

Wann entschied Berta sich, eine künstlerische Laufbahn einzuschlagen?

Ich kam zwei Jahre nach Berta auf die Höhere Mädchenschule in Simbach, und kurz nach meinem Eintritt dürfte diese Entscheidung gefallen sein. Berta war lange hin- und hergerissen zwischen der Überlegung, Turnlehrerin zu werden und einer künstlerischen Ausbildung. Wahrscheinlich war die Tatsache, dass ich im Turnen besser war als sie, auch zu einem gewissen Grad ausschlaggebend. Am Ende bin ja auch ich Turnlehrin geworden und sie ging auf die Kunstgewerbeschule.

Bertas großes künstlerisches Talent wurde schon früh sichtbar. Förderte man sie in der Schule und in der Familie?

Schon in der Massinger Volksschule war Berta so etwas wie eine »kleine Berühmtheit«, jeder kannte sie und bewunderte ihr Können. »Hummel Bertl, zeichne mich!« war ein oft vorgebrachter Wunsch der Schulkameraden, der mir noch heute in den Ohren klingt. In der Höheren Mädchenschule in Simbach durfte Berta außerhalb der normalen Unterrichtszeiten den Zeichensaal benutzen, das war etwas ganz besonderes. Damals entstand unter anderem das Ölgemälde »Segelschiff«.

   Das Wohlwollen der Familie äußerte sich vor allem darin, dass man Berta den Weg in die Münchener Kunstgewerbeschule ebnete und sie in jeder Hinsicht unterstützte. Es war für diese Zeit absolut außergewöhnlich, dass ein Mädchen vom Land eine solche Ausbildung in München begann. Unser Vater hat sehr an Berta geglaubt und sie damals sogar zur Aufnahmeprüfung in München begleitet. Sie bestand diese Prüfung ohne besondere Vorbereitung als eine der Besten, sie hat sie regelrecht »aus dem Ärmel geschüttelt«. Mir hat sie später erzählt, dass eine der Aufgaben darin bestand, einen Mann zu zeichnen, der vor den Prüflingen hin und her ging.

Sailing ship/Segelschiff
1926/27, oil on canvas/Öl auf Lw, 26 × 34 $^1/_2$ in./660 × 875 mm
HM 471

Die erste Zeit in München war für Berta nicht immer einfach. Sie standen in engem Kontakt zu Ihrer Schwester, hat sie Ihnen über ihre Anfangsschwierigkeiten berichtet?

Die Probleme, die Berta zunächst in München hatte, bezogen sich eigentlich nur auf ihre äußeren Umstände und nicht auf ihr Studium an der Kunstgewerbeschule. Ihre erste Zimmerwirtin hat ihr das Leben recht schwer gemacht, Berta hat sich in ihrer Bleibe nicht wohl gefühlt. Außerdem gab sie ihr ganzes Geld für Farbe aus und hatte meist nichts mehr übrig, um sich etwas zu Essen zu kaufen. Schließlich lernte Berta zwei Klosterschwestern aus Sießen kennen, die ebenfalls an der Kunstgewerbeschule studierten und ihr zu einem Zimmer in einem Schwesternwohnheim in der Blumenstraße verhalfen. Von da an verlief die Studienzeit sehr harmonisch und ich weiß noch, dass sie oft Ausstellungen besucht und das kulturelle Leben sehr genossen hat.

Ihre Ferien verbrachte Berta hauptsächlich in Massing bei der Familie. Wie haben Sie sie in dieser Zeit erlebt?

Die Ferienaufenthalte bei der Familie waren sicher ein wichtiger und schöner Ausgleich zum Studium in München. Berta hat auch in diesen freien Tagen viel gemalt und gezeichnet. Wenn sie aus München heimgekommen ist, ist meist keine Viertelstunde vergangen und der Vater hat gesagt: »Du Berta, ich hab' wieder einen schönen Charakterkopf für dich, da fahr' ich dich hin.« So kam es zu den zahlreichen Porträtstudien von Bauern und Bäuerinnen aus dem Massinger Umland. Unser Hund, der Boxer »Lord«, der hatte es ihr auch angetan, zu dem hatte sie eine enge Beziehung. Dementsprechend oft ist er in ihren Werken aus diesen Jahren zu finden.

In schöner Erinnerung habe ich auch die wundervollen Dekorationen, die Berta zusammen mit dem Vater für unser Geschäft gestaltete, da gab es Hexenhäuschen, eine Mühle, die sich bewegte und vieles mehr. Speziell zu Weihnachten haben sich die beiden immer gemeinsam eine Auslage überlegt und umgesetzt, der Vater war da sehr einfallsreich. Die Kinder sind regelmäßig draußen vor dem Fenster gestanden und haben sich die Nasen plattgedrückt.

Zahlreiche Werke mit landschaftlichen Motiven entstanden ebenfalls in dieser Zeit. Durch Bertas Bilder gewinnt man einen guten Eindruck, wie Massing und die umliegenden Dörfer damals aussahen – Fotografien existieren ja kaum. Berta hat mich oft mitgenommen und ich habe ihr beim Malen zugesehen oder mich mit Stickereien beschäftigt. Meist versuchte sie, mich auch zum Malen zu motivieren. »Schau her Centa, so entsteht ein Bild«, sagte sie bei diesen Gelegenheiten. Einmal, wir besuchten gemeinsam eine Tante in der Pfalz, habe ich tatsächlich eine Burgruine gemalt. Letztendlich traute ich mich aber nicht, sie ihr zu zeigen.

Wann hat sich in Berta der Wunsch manifestiert, ins Kloster zu gehen? Haben sie von diesem Entscheidungsprozess etwas mitbekommen?

Die schon erwähnten beiden Klosterschwestern aus Sießen kamen später als Berta an die Münchener Kunstgewerbeschule, und Berta wurde von ihrem Professor Maximilian Dasio gebeten, sich als Obmännin um die Neuankömmlinge zu kümmern. Sicher hat dieser enge Kontakt dazu beigetragen, Berta mit dem Klosterleben vertraut zu machen. Über die eigentliche Entscheidung, ins Kloster zu gehen, sprach Berta nicht, sie hat das im Stillen mit sich ausgemacht. In der Familie wurde dieser Schritt akzeptiert, ohne groß darüber zu reden.

Anders war das an ihrer Schule in München. Nach ihrem Abschluss, den sie übrigens als Beste der Klasse bestand, bot ihr Professor Dasio eine Stelle als Lehrkraft an, aber Berta lehnte sie ab, weil sie sich für das Kloster entschieden hatte. Dasio war darüber tief enttäuscht und wandte sich von Berta ab, wir haben aber später erfahren, dass er ihren weiteren Weg sehr genau verfolgte, ohne je wieder persönlichen Kontakt aufzunehmen. Ganz anders ging Professorin Else Brauneis, die ebenfalls große Stücke auf Berta gehalten hatte, damit um. Sie unterstützte Berta weiterhin und brach auch die Verbindung zu ihr nicht ab.

Die Familie hat das Werk Bertas sehr sorgfältig gesammelt und verwaltet. War hier auch Ihr Vater ausschlaggebend?

Auf alle Fälle! Unser Vater war generell ein passionierter Sammler und hatte schon einen entsprechenden Ruf in Massing. Wenn jemand etwas schönes gefunden hatte, seien es alte Waffen oder ein Mammutzahn, hieß es nur: »Bring es zum Hummel!« Genauso verfuhr er mit Bertas Zeichnungen und Gemälden: Er bewahrte von der ersten Postkarte an, die sie bemalt hatte, wirklich jedes Blatt auf, hielt die Sachen auch nach ihrem Tod zusammen und legte damit den Grundstock für die heutige Sammlung. Auch die nächsten Generationen nahmen sich der Werke an, bis diese schließlich ihren Platz im eigens gegründeten Museum gefunden haben. Uns ist heute besonders wichtig, den zahlreichen Liebhabern der Hummel-Figuren auch diese weitgehend unbekannte Seite Berta Hummels zu zeigen.

Können Sie abschließend noch etwas zur Persönlichkeit Ihrer Schwester sagen? Was war sie für ein Mensch, wie haben Sie Berta in Erinnerung?

Berta war eine sehr positive, lebensbejahende und temperamentvolle, fast stürmische Person. Sie liebte Kinder über alles, was ja aus ihrem Werk klar hervorgeht, und besaß einen besonderen Humor, der sich beispielsweise in Ihren Karikaturen widerspiegelt. Sie hatte eine schnelle Auffassungsgabe und traf mit Ihren Zeichnungen und Gemälden – vor allem mit den Porträts – genau den Punkt, konnte einen gewissen Charakter, eine gewisse Stimmung exakt einfangen. Das ist eine Gabe, die sehr selten ist und die ich über alle Maßen an ihr bewundert habe.

Berta Hummel
Stationen ihres Lebens

21. Mai 1909
Berta Hummel wird in Massing an der Rott geboren

1. Mai 1915
Einschulung an der Massinger Volksschule

3. Mai 1921
Übertritt in das Institut Marienhöhe in Simbach am Inn, eine Höhere Mädchenschule der Englischen Fräulein

25. März 1926
Abschluss der Ausbildung im Institut Marienhöhe

1927–1931
Studium an der Staatsschule für angewandte Kunst (umbenannt 1928) bei den Professoren Maximilian Dasio, Else Brauneis, Friedrich Wirnhier und anderen; Freundschaft mit zwei jungen Franziskanerinnen aus dem Kloster Sießen bei Saulgau/Württemberg, die ebenfalls an der Staatsschule studieren

18. März 1931
Abschlussprüfung an der Staatsschule für angewandte Kunst in München hervorragend bestanden, Abschlusszeugnis mit der Gesamtnote »Eins«

22. April 1931
Eintritt in das Franziskanerinnenkloster Sießen als Kandidatin; dort vor allem in der Paramentenwerkstatt und als Zeichenlehrerin tätig; Kinderbilder, Auftragsarbeiten

ab 1931
Jährliche Ausstellungen in Sießen, auch in Beuron und München

Dezember 1932
Erster Druck von Bildern und Postkarten in Rottenburg und München

30. Mai–8. Juni 1933
Letzter Besuch im Elternhaus vor der Einkleidung im Kloster Sießen

22. August 1933
Einkleidung, Annahme des Namens Maria Innocentia, Beginn des einjährigen Noviziates

ab 1933
Dauerausstellung im »Hummelsaal« des Klosters Sießen

Berta at the age of two, 1910/11
Die zweijährige Berta, 1910/11

Sister Maria Innocentia Hummel OSF, 1934
Schwester Maria Innocentia Hummel OSF, 1934

30. August 1934
Profess, öffentliche Ablegung der ersten Gelübde

4. November 1934
Erscheinen des ersten »Hummel-Buches« im Verlag Emil Fink, Stuttgart, Auflage 5.000 Stück

1934/35
Erste Verbindung zur Porzellanfabrik Goebel in Oeslau, heute Rödental, bei Coburg; Beginn mit der Produktion von »Hummel-Figuren«

1935
Erstausstellung der Hummel-Figuren auf der Leipziger Frühjahrsmesse

5. Mai 1935
Beginn eines Aufbaustudiums an der Staatsschule für angewandte Kunst in München

18.–20. August 1936
Besichtigung der Porzellanfabrik Goebel in Oeslau; Dank der Arbeiter an Schwester Maria Innocentia für die Arbeitsbeschaffung durch die Produktion der Hummel-Figuren

23. März 1937
Angriff der Nationalsozialisten auf die Kinderbilder Schwester Maria Innocentias in der Zeitschrift »Der SA-Mann«

24. April 1937
Nach krankheitsbedingter Unterbrechung Abschluss des Zweitstudiums an der Staatsschule für angewandte Kunst in München, wiederum mit der Gesamtnote »Eins«

30. August 1937
Ewige Profess, Ablegung der Gelübde auf Lebenszeit

9. April 1938
Eintreffen des Altarblattes mit der Darstellung Bruder Konrads für Massing, Aufstellung am linken Seitenaltar der Pfarrkirche

Oktober 1939
Erscheinen des zweiten Hummel-Buches »Hui, die Hummel« im Verlag »Ars sacra« Josef Müller, München

4. November 1940
Räumung des Klosters Sießen auf Anordnung der nationalsozialistischen Machthaber

November 1940 und Oktober 1942
Erholungsaufenthalte bei den Eltern in Massing

August 1944–September 1945
Aufenthalte in den Lungenheilstätten Isny und Wangen

9. September 1946
Rückkehr ins Kloster Sießen

6. November 1946
Tod von Schwester Maria Innocentia Hummel im Kloster Sießen

9. November 1946

Beerdigung auf dem Klosterfriedhof in Sießen

20.–24. August 1947

Ausstellung von Werken Schwester Maria Innocentias im Gasthof Anglsperger in Massing

17.–25. April 1948

Kulturausstellung der Stadt Friedrichshafen mit Werken von Schwester Maria Innocentia Hummel

Oktober 1950

Ausstellung in Massing von Hummel-Bildern und Hummel-Figuren zusammen mit der Sammlung A. Hummel

1978

Einrichtung des jetzigen Hummelsaales im Kloster Sießen mit Kinderbildern, Altarbildern und den Kreuzweg-Skizzen

1978

Eröffnung des Berta-Hummel-Museums in Massing; große Sammlung alter und neuer Hummel-Figuren

1980–1982

Wanderausstellung durch verschiedene Städte der USA »Formation of an Artist« (frühe Werke von Berta Hummel)

Juli–Oktober 1985

50 Jahre M.I. Hummel-Figuren 1935-1985 im Museum der Deutschen Porzellanindustrie Hohenberg a.d. Eger

August 1985

Ausstellung »Die andere Berta Hummel« anlässlich der Eröffnung der Berta-Hummel-Volksschule in Massing

6. November 1986–1. Februar 1987

Ausstellung im Diözesanmuseum Obermünster Regensburg »Die andere Berta Hummel – Unbekannte Werke einer bekannten Künstlerin«

Oktober 1993

Eröffnung des Hummel-Museums in New Braunfels, Texas, USA

22. Juli 1994

Einweihung des neuen »Berta-Hummel-Museums im Hummelhaus« (Geburtshaus) in Massing

6. November 1996

Eröffnung der Ausstellung »Letztes Schenken« zum 50. Todestag der Künstlerin im Berta-Hummel-Museum im Hummelhaus in Massing

21. Mai 1999

Eröffnung der Ausstellung »Frohes Beginnen« zum 90. Geburtstag der Künstlerin im Berta-Hummel-Museum im Hummelhaus

27. Juni 2000

Eröffnung der Ausstellung »Massing und Berta Hummel« im Berta-Hummel-Museum im Hummelhaus anlässlich der 650 Jahr-Feier der Markterhebung Massings sowie des Jubiläums 125 Jahre Familie Hummel in Massing

27. Juni 2001

Eröffnung der Ausstellung »Die Farbe der Erinnerung«, Gedächtnisausstellung zum 50. Geburtstag der Museumsgründerin Maria Hummel im Berta-Hummel-Museum im Hummelhaus

4. Juni 2002

Ausstellungseröffnung »Neuentdeckungen und Neuerwerbungen« im Berta-Hummel-Museum im Hummelhaus

PLATES
TAFELTEIL

Berta Hummel, self-portrait/Selbstporträt Berta Hummel
1929, red chalk/Rötel, 10 × 7 $^{1}/_{4}$ in./252 × 187 mm
HM 514

Child reading/Lesendes Kind
1928, watercolor/Wasserfarbe, 5 $\frac{1}{4}$ × 6 $\frac{1}{2}$ in./130 × 165 mm
HM 50

Massing, market square in winter/Massing, Marktplatz im Winter
1928.12, pencil/Bleistift, 9 $\frac{1}{4}$ × 12 $\frac{1}{2}$ in./235 × 320 mm
HM 618

Massing, Berta-Hummel-Straße
1929.04, watercolor/Aquarell, 12 $\frac{1}{4}$ × 9 in./310 × 230 mm
HM 652

Massing, old houses/Massing, alte Häuser
1929/30, watercolor/Aquarell, 17 $\frac{1}{4}$ × 13 in./440 × 330 mm
HM 864a

Market in Munich/München, Viktualienmarkt
1929/30, watercolor/Aquarell, 10 × 13 $\frac{1}{4}$ in./251 × 348 mm
HM 265

Over the roofs/Über den Dächern
1928/30, watercolor/Aquarell, 9 $^1/_2$ × 15 $^3/_4$ in./235 × 400 mm
HM 352

Red dahlias/Rote Dahlien
1929/30, watercolor/Aquarell, 16 $\frac{1}{4}$ × 11 $\frac{3}{4}$ in./415 × 298 mm
HM 532

Poinsettia/Weihnachtsstern
1928/30, watercolor/Aquarell, 19 ¹/₂ × 13 ³/₄ in./498 × 348 mm
HM 838a

Campanula in vase/Glockenblumen im Krug
1929/30, watercolor/Aquarell, 20 $^1/_4$ × 14 $^3/_4$ in./518 × 375 mm
HM 892

Crucifix with flowers/Kruzifix mit Blüten
1929/30, watercolor/Aquarell, 21 1/4 × 13 3/4 in./537 × 348 mm
HM 839

Statue between candles/Standbild zwischen zwei Kerzen
1929/30, watercolor/Aquarell, 12 $\frac{3}{4}$ × 8 $\frac{1}{4}$ in./322 × 213 mm
HM 868

Living room with house-altar/Stube mit Herrgotts-Winkel

1929/30, watercolor/Aquarell, 13 $^3/_4$ × 18 in./352 × 457 mm

HM 943

Girls in ethnic costume/Mädchen in Tracht
1929/30, watercolor/Aquarell, 11 $\frac{1}{2}$ × 9 $\frac{1}{4}$ in./290 × 235 mm
HM 196a

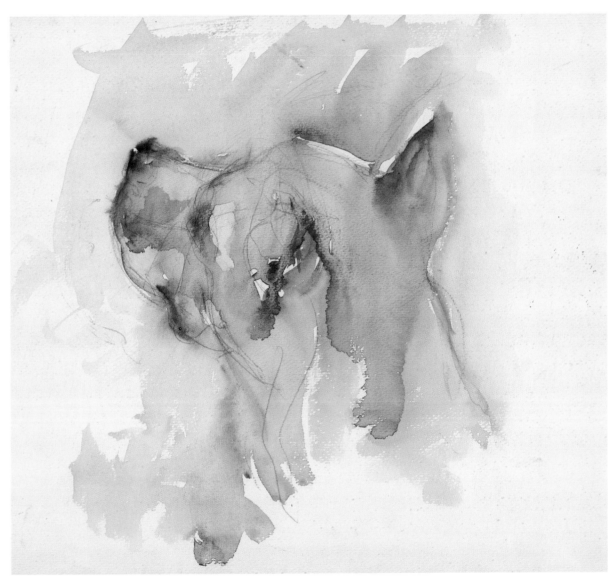

The dog "Lord"/Der Hund »Lord«
1929/30, watercolor/Aquarell, 13 $^1/_2$ × 13 $^1/_2$ in./340 × 340 mm
HM 210

Portrait of Professor Else Brauneis/Porträt Else Brauneis
1930, watercolor, pencil/Aquarell, Bleistift, 10 $^3/_4$ × 7 $^1/_4$ in./270 × 187 mm
HM 142a

Portrait of Professor Maximilian Dasio, reading the newspaper/Porträt Maximilian Dasio, Zeitung lesend
1930, watercolor/Aquarell, 10 $^1/_2$ × 7 $^1/_2$ in./268 × 188 mm
HM 157

Portrait of a man with wide-brimmed hat/Porträt Mann mit Hut
1929/30, pastel chalk/Pastell, 13 $^1/_4$ × 10 $^1/_2$ in./335 × 265 mm
HM 531

Portrait of a peasant woman/Porträt einer Bäuerin
1929/30, charcoal/Kohle, 10 $\frac{1}{4}$ × 7 $\frac{1}{2}$ in./260 × 188 mm
HM 145a

Portrait of an old man/Porträt eines Greises
1930, charcoal/Kohle, 15 $^3/_4$ × 10 $^1/_4$ in./400 × 260 mm
HM 229

Margret, seated/Margret, sitzend
1930, charcoal/Kohle, 12 $\frac{1}{4}$ × 6 $\frac{1}{2}$ in./310 × 165 mm
KS Q

Peasant woman with head-scarf/Bäuerin mit Kopftuch
1929, watercolor/Aquarell, 10 3/4 × 18 1/2 in./272 × 468 mm
HM 479b

Peasant with hat/Bauer mit Hut
1930, watercolor/Aquarell, 19 ³/₄ × 12 ³/₄ in./502 × 327 mm
HM 938a

Massing, Corpus Christi Procession/Massing, Prozession
1931, crayon, pencil/Farbstift, Bleistift, 8 $\frac{1}{4}$ × 10 $\frac{3}{4}$ in./210 × 270 mm
HM 886

Massing, cattle market/Massing, Viehmarkt
1931, crayon, pencil/Farbstift, Bleistift, 8 $\frac{1}{4}$ × 11 $\frac{1}{4}$ in./210 × 285 mm
HM 885A

Lady in red/Dame in Rot
1930, watercolor, pencil/Aquarell, Bleistift, 19 $^3/_4$ × 11 in./500 × 280 mm
HM 239

INDEX OF WORKS
WERKVERZEICHNIS

1

4

2

5

3

6

1 **Fairy tale garden/Kleine Figur im Märchengarten**
1927, pencil/Bleistift, 1 ³/₄ × 2 in./45 × 49 mm
Privat

2 **Boy with sunflowers (woodcut design)/Bub mit Sonnenblumen (Entwurf zu Holzschnitt HM 630)**
1927, pen and ink/Tusche, 3 ¹/₂ × 2 ³/₄ in./90 × 70 mm
HM 639

3 **Boy with sunflowers/Bub mit Sonnenblumen**
1927, woodcut/Holzschnitt, 4 × 2 ³/₄ in./100 × 72 mm
HM 630

4 **Birthday greetings/Zum Geburtstag**
1927, woodcut/Holzschnitt, 3 ¹/₂ × 2 ¹/₂ in./80 × 110 mm
HM 637

5 **Christmas card/Weihnachtskarte**
1927, woodcut/Holzschnitt, 2 ³/₄ × 3 in./70 × 75 mm
HM 633

6 **Toadstool/Fliegenpilz**
1927, woodcut/Holzschnitt, 3 ¹/₄ × 4 ¹/₄ in./90 × 65 mm
HM 638*

7

10

8

11

9

7   **Head study of a young man/Kopfstudie eines jungen Mannes**
1927, red chalk/Rötel, 9 $^1/_2$ × 7 $^1/_4$ in./240 × 183 mm
HM 130

8   **Adalbero Hugo with Maria Hugo/P. Adalbero Hugo mit Maria Hugo**
1927, charcoal/Kohle, 9 $^1/_2$ × 7 $^1/_4$ in./245 × 185 mm
HM 415

9   **Portrait of the Hugo cousins/Porträt der drei Hugo Kinder**
1927, charcoal/Kohle, 9 $^1/_2$ × 7 $^1/_4$ in./245 × 160 mm
HM 417

10 **Portrait of Maria Anglsperger/Porträt Maria Anglsperger**
1927, watercolor, pen and ink/Wasserfarbe, Tusche,
9 $^1/_2$ × 6 $^1/_4$ in./230 × 184 mm
HM 413

11 **Siesta (Uncle Alois)/Onkel Alois beim Mittagsschlaf**
1927, charcoal/Kohle, 9 × 7 $^1/_4$ in./245 × 185 mm
HM 416

12

15

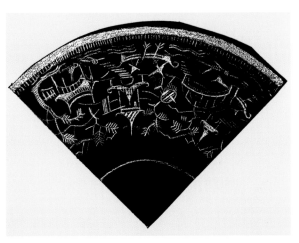

13

12 **Portrait of Kreszentia Anglsperger/Porträt Kreszentia Anglsperger**
1927, Pittchalk/Pittkreide, 13 $^3/_4$ × 11 $^3/_4$ in./350 × 300 mm
HM 526

13 **Chinoiserie**
1927, crayon/Farbstift, 9 $^1/_4$ × 6 in./143 × 202 mm
HM 12

14 **Colour study/Farbstudie**
1927, crayon/Farbstift, 5 $^1/_2$ × 8 in./76 × 76 mm
HM 13

15 **Portrait of Viktoria Hummel/Porträt Viktoria Hummel**
1927.04, pencil/Bleistift, 3 × 3 in./235 × 153 mm
HM 900

16 **Peacock/Pfau**
1927, watercolor/Wasserfarbe, 4 $^1/_4$ × 4 $^1/_4$ in./107 × 108 mm
HM 15

14

16

17

19

18

20

21

17 Wallpaper for children/Kindertapete
1927, pencil/Bleistift, 3 ³/₄ × 3 ³/₄ in./93 × 94 mm
HM 16

18 Wallpaper for children/Kindertapete
1927, pencil, watercolor/Bleistift, Wasserfarbe,
2 ¹/₂ × 3 ³/₄ in./61 × 95 mm
HM 17

19 Wallpaper for children/Kindertapete
1927, pencil, crayon/Bleistift, Farbstift,
1 ¹/₄ × 2 ³/₄ in./90 × 105 mm
HM 18

20 Wallpaper for children/Kindertapete
1927, pencil/Bleistift, 7 ³/₄ × 5 in./30 × 67 mm
HM 19

21 The red mitten/Der rote Fäustling
1927, crayon/Farbstift, 3 ¹/₂ × 4 ¹/₄ in./200 × 125 mm
HM 469

22

23

25

24

26

27

27 **Wildflowers in yellow jug/Feldblumen im Krug**
1927, watercolor/Aquarell, 12 $^3/_4$ × 19 in./325 × 483 mm
HM 325b

28 **Daisies and anemones in blue vase/Margeriten und Anemonen in blauer Vase**
1927/28, watercolor/Aquarell, 18 $^1/_2$ × 14 $^1/_4$ in./470 × 365 mm
HM 257

29 **Flowers in brown vase/Blumen in brauner Vase**
1927/28, watercolor/Aquarell, 23 × 16 $^1/_2$ in./584 × 422 mm
HM 258

29

28

30

32

31

33

30 **Roses/Rosen**
    1927/28, pencil/Bleistift, 8 $^1/_4$ × 6 $^1/_4$ in./210 × 162 mm
    HM 179

31 **Roses/Rosen**
    1927/28, pencil/Bleistift, 8 $^1/_4$ × 6 $^1/_4$ in./210 × 162 mm
    HM 180

32 **Daisies/Margeriten**
    1927/28, pencil/Bleistift, 8 $^1/_4$ × 6 $^1/_4$ in./210 × 162 mm
    HM 181

33 **Pelargoniums/Pelargonien**
    1927/28, pencil/Bleistift, 8 $^1/_4$ × 6 $^1/_4$ in./210 × 162 mm
    HM 182

34

37

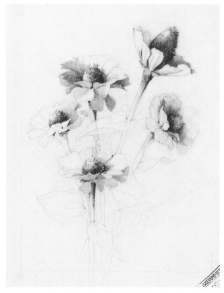

35

38

36

34 **Narcissi/Narzissen**
    1927/28, pencil/Bleistift, 8 $^1/_4$ × 6 $^1/_4$ in./210 × 162 mm
    HM 183

35 **Zinnias/Zinnien**
    1927/28, pencil/Bleistift, 8 $^1/_4$ × 6 $^1/_4$ in./210 × 162 mm
    HM 184

36 **Zinnias/Zinnien**
    1927/28, pencil/Bleistift, 9 $^1/_4$ × 6 $^1/_4$ in./235 × 162 mm
    HM 185

37 **Gladiolae/Gladiole**
    1927/28, pencil/Bleistift, 10 $^1/_2$ × 6 $^1/_2$ in./270 × 165 mm
    HM 186

38 **Daisies/Margeriten**
    1927/28, pencil/Bleistift, 8 $^1/_4$ × 6 $^1/_4$ in./210 × 162 mm
    HM 187

39

40

41 Begonias/Begonien
1927/28, pencil/Bleistift, 8 $^1/_4$ × 6 $^1/_4$ in./210 × 162 mm
HM 190

42 Cosmea/Cosmea
1927/28, pencil/Bleistift, 7 $^3/_4$ × 6 $^1/_4$ in./200 × 162 mm
HM 191

41

42

39 Daffodils/Osterglocken
1927/28, pencil/Bleistift, 7 $^3/_4$ × 6 $^1/_4$ in./195 × 160 mm
HM 188

40 Daisies/Margeriten
1927/28, pencil/Bleistift, 8 $^1/_4$ × 6 $^1/_4$ in./210 × 162 mm
HM 189

43

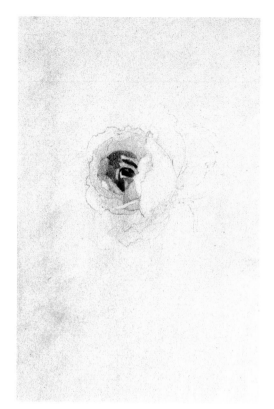

45

44

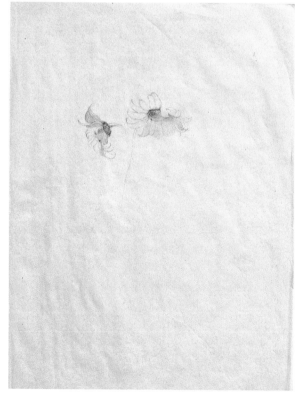

46

43 **Flower (fragment)/Blüte (Fragment)**
1927/28, pencil/Bleistift, 6 × 4 $^3/_4$ in./150 × 120 mm
HM 545

44 **Lily (fragment)/Lilie (Fragment)**
1927/28, pencil/Bleistift, 9 $^3/_4$ × 7 $^1/_2$ in./250 × 190 mm
HM 591

45 **Rose (fragment)/Rose (Fragment)**
1927/28, pencil/Bleistift, 3 $^1/_4$ × 3 in./80 × 75 mm
Privat

46 **Daisies (fragment)/Margeriten (Fragment)**
1927/28, pencil/Bleistift, 4 $^1/_2$ × 4 in./105 × 100 mm
Privat

47

50

48

47 **Anemones/Anemonen**
1927/28, pencil/Bleistift, 7 $^3/_4$ × 6 in./200 × 150 mm
KS A

48 **Daisies/Margeriten**
1927/28, pencil/Bleistift, 12 $^1/_2$ × 10 $^1/_4$ in./320 × 260 mm
KS B

49 **Textile design/Entwurf für Stoffdruck**
1927/28, woodcut/Holzschnitt, 11 $^3/_4$ × 9 $^1/_2$ in./158 × 135 mm
KS D

50 **Daisies and narcissi/Margeriten und Narzissen**
1927/28, pencil/Bleistift, 6 $^1/_4$ × 5 $^1/_4$ in./300 × 240 mm
KS C

51 **Textile design/Entwurf für Stoffdruck**
1927/28, woodcut/Holzschnitt, 5 $^1/_2$ × 5 $^3/_4$ in./140 × 146 mm
HM 468

51

49

52

52 Marienhöhe, school institute in Simbach/Simbach, Marienhöhe
1927/28, lithograph/Lithographie, 10 × 6 $^3/_4$ in./251 × 171 mm
HM 568

53 Anzenberg, interior of church/Anzenberg, Innenansicht der Kirche
1927/28, crayon/Farbstift, 8 $^3/_4$ × 7 $^3/_4$ in./225 × 195 mm
HM 610

54 Massing, parish church interior/Massing, Innenansicht der Pfarrkirche
1927/28, watercolor/Aquarell, 11 × 8 $^3/_4$ in./281 × 221 mm
HM 611

54

53

55

55 Portrait of Centa Hummel/Porträt Centa Hummel
1927/28, graphite/Graphit, 9 $^1/_2$ × 7 $^1/_4$ in./240 × 183 mm
HM 430

56 Portrait of Maria Anglsperger/Porträt Maria Anglsperger
1927/28, pen and ink, charcoal/Tusche, Kohle,
11 × 15 in./280 × 380 mm
HM 213

57 Portrait of Maria Angslperger/Porträt Maria Anglsperger
1927/28, charcoal/Kohle, 11 $^3/_4$ × 7 $^3/_4$ in./300 × 200 mm
HM 427

58 Portrait of a boy/Porträt eines Knaben
1927/28, graphite/Graphit, 10 $^1/_2$ × 7 $^1/_2$ in./270 × 190 mm
HM 127

56

57

58

59

61

62

60

60 **Young woman, seated/Frau auf einem Stuhl sitzend**
1927/28, charcoal/Kohle, 9 $^3/_4$ × 6 $^3/_4$ in./377 × 235 mm
HM 242

61 **Portrait of a woman/Porträt einer Frau**
1927/28, charcoal/Kohle, 12 × 8 $^1/_4$ in./305 × 210 mm
HM 133

59 **Portrait of a woman/Porträt einer Frau**
1927/28, graphite/Graphit, 11 $^3/_4$ × 17 $^1/_4$ in./300 × 435 mm
HM 465

62 **Portrait of a young woman/Porträt einer jungen Frau**
1927/28, charcoal/Kohle, 14 $^3/_4$ × 9 $^1/_4$ in./250 × 172 mm
HM 135

63

63 Peasant woman with basket, seated/Bäuerin mit Korb, sitzend
1927/28, charcoal/Kohle, 12 $\frac{1}{4}$ × 7 $\frac{1}{4}$ in./310 × 186 mm
HM 202a

64 Peasant woman, seated/Bäuerin, sitzend
1927/28, charcoal/Kohle, cropped/beschnitten
HM 202b

65 Man reading a newspaper/Sitzender Mann, Zeitung lesend
1927/28, charcoal/Kohle, 13 × 7 $\frac{1}{4}$ in./330 × 185 mm
HM 203

66 Little girl, reclining/Kleines Mädchen, liegend
1927/28, crayon/Farbstift, 7 × 4 $\frac{3}{4}$ in./180 × 120 mm
HM 53

65

64

66

67

68

70

67 **Still life with lobster/Stillleben mit Hummer**
1927/28, watercolor/Aquarell, 15 $^1/_4$ × 13 $^1/_2$ in./390 × 340 mm
HM 259

68 **Still life with large white jug/Stillleben mit großem weißen Krug**
1927/28, watercolor/Aquarell, 12 × 16 $^1/_4$ in./306 × 413 mm
HM 845b

69 **Twigs/Zweige**
1927/30, pencil/Bleistift, 19 $^3/_4$ × 15 in./230 × 170 mm
HM 592

70 **Still life with red vase/Stillleben mit roter Vase**
1927/29, watercolor/Aquarell, 9 × 6 $^3/_4$ in./500 × 380 mm
HM 337

71 **Pulsatilla/Küchenschelle**
1927/30, pen and ink/Tusche, 8 $^1/_2$ × 7 $^1/_2$ in./220 × 190 mm
HM 593

69

71

72

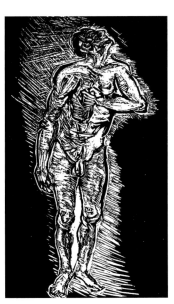

73

75

72 **Seefeld**
1927/30, pencil/Bleistift, 7 $^1/_4$ × 6 $^3/_4$ in./186 × 174 mm
HM 524

73 **Male nude, standing/Männlicher Akt, stehend**
1927/30, woodcut/Holzschnitt, 6 $^3/_4$ × 4 $^1/_4$ in./174 × 105 mm
HM 569

74 **Female nude, recumbent/Weiblicher Akt, liegend**
1927/30, charcoal/Kohle, 7 $^3/_4$ × 15 $^1/_4$ in./196 × 386 mm
HM 276

75 **Male nude/Männlicher Akt, Halbrückenansicht**
1927/30, red chalk/Rötel, 18 $^1/_4$ × 7 $^3/_4$ in./464 × 200 mm
HM 279

74

76

76-80 Window decorations, Christmas 1928
Schaufensterdekorationen für
Weihnachten 1928
HM 451/1-3

77

76-80 **Window decorations, Christmas 1928
Schaufensterdekorationen für
Weihnachten 1928**
HM 451/1-3

76 **Flying angels/Engel über einer Landschaft**
1928, watercolor/Wasserfarbe, 26 ¹/₄ × 59 ³/₄ in./670 × 1520 mm
HM 451/1

77 **Christ Child riding on a lama/Christkind auf Lama mit Engeln**
1928, watercolor/Wasserfarbe, 8 × 9 ¹/₄ in./204 × 237 mm
HM 451/2

79 **Two girls/Zwei Mädchen**
1928, watercolor/Wasserfarbe, 4 ³/₄ × 2 ¹/₂ in./120 × 65 mm
HM 451/3

79 **Mother and children/Mutter mit Kindern**
1928, watercolor/Wasserfarbe, 10 ³/₄ × 9 ¹/₄ in./272 × 237 mm
HM 450

80 **Santa Claus/Weihnachtsmann**
1928, watercolor/Wasserfarbe, 37 ³/₄ × 20 ¹/₂ in./960 × 525 mm
HM 452

78   79   80

81

83

82

84

81 **Child reading/Lesendes Kind**
1928, watercolor/Wasserfarbe, 5 $\frac{1}{4}$ × 6 $\frac{1}{2}$ in./130 × 165 mm
HM 50

82 **Easter card I/Ostergrußkarte I**
1928, woodcut/Holzschnitt, 2 $\frac{1}{2}$ × 2 $\frac{1}{2}$ in./65 × 65 mm
HM 634

83 **Certificate, Simbach school 1928/Absolvia Simbach 1928**
1928, woodcut/Holzschnitt, 5 $\frac{1}{2}$ × 3 $\frac{1}{2}$ in./138 × 90 mm
HM 445

84 **Easter card II/Ostergrußkarte II**
1928, colored woodcut/Holzschnitt, koloriert,
3 $\frac{1}{2}$ × 3 $\frac{1}{4}$ in./90 × 85 mm
HM 635

85

88

85 **Portrait of Katharina Hummel/Porträt Katharina Hummel**
1928, graphite/Graphit, 4 $\frac{1}{4}$ × 2 $\frac{3}{4}$ in./105 × 73 mm
HM 822a

86 **Portrait of Viki Hummel/Porträt Viki Hummel**
1928, charcoal/Kohle, 12 $\frac{1}{4}$ × 9 $\frac{1}{4}$ in./310 × 235 mm
HM 428

87 **Portrait of a man (fragment)/Porträt eines Mannes (Fragment)**
1928, graphite/Graphit, cropped/beschnitten
HM 905b

88 **Portrait of a woman/Porträt einer Frau**
1928, charcoal/Kohle, 14 $\frac{1}{4}$ × 11 $\frac{1}{2}$ in./360 × 293 mm
HM 220

86

87

89

92

90

93

91

89 **Portrait of a man/Porträt eines Mannes**
1928, graphite/Graphit, 12 $^1/_2$ × 10 $^1/_2$ in./315 × 265 mm
HM 153

90 **Portrait of Georg Anglsperger/Porträt Georg Anglsperger**
1928, graphite/Graphit, 8 $^3/_4$ × 7 in./225 × 175 mm
HM 904

91 **Portrait of a young woman/Porträt einer jungen Frau**
1928, charcoal/Kohle, 10 $^1/_2$ × 7 $^1/_2$ in./268 × 188 mm
HM 132

92 **Head study of a woman/Kopfstudie einer jungen Frau**
1928, charcoal/Kohle, 11 $^3/_4$ × 9 $^1/_4$ in./298 × 234 mm
HM 828

93 **Portrait of an old woman/Porträt einer alten Frau**
1928, charcoal/Kohle, 13 × 7 $^3/_4$ in./330 × 195 mm
HM 144

94

97

95

98

96

94 Portrait of Centa Hummel/Porträt Centa Hummel mit Absolvia-Mütze
1928, crayon/Farbstift, 11 ³/₄ × 11 in./300 × 278 mm
HM 419

95 Three Anglsperger sisters/Porträt drei Schwestern Anglsperger
1928.04, graphite/Graphit, 10 ³/₄ × 16 ¹/₄ in./272 × 410 mm
HM 905a

96 Little girl with basket/Kind mit Korb
1928, red chalk/Rötel, 9 × 4 ³/₄ in./230 × 120 mm
HM 54

97 Portrait of a woman/Porträt einer Frau
1928, watercolor/Aquarell, 14 ¹/₄ × 10 ¹/₂ in./360 × 266 mm
HM 519

98 Portrait of Lotte Anglsperger/Porträt Lotte Anglsperger
1928, watercolor/Aquarell, 13 × 9 ³/₄ in./330 × 250 mm
HM 903a

99

99 **Berta Hummel, self-portrait/Selbstporträt Berta Hummel**
1928, pencil/Bleistift, 12 $^1/_2$ × 8 $^3/_4$ in./320 × 220 mm
HM 432

100 **Portrait of a young woman/Porträt einer jungen Frau**
1928, graphite/Graphit, 9 $^1/_4$ × 7 in./237 × 179 mm
HM 136

101 **Portrait of Maria Hugo/Porträt Maria Hugo**
1928 1928 dated/datiert, red chalk/Rötel,
7 $^1/_2$ × 7 $^1/_2$ in./192 × 190 mm
HM 946

102 **Portrait of Ruth Hugo/Porträt Ruth Hugo**
1928, red chalk/Rötel, 10 $^1/_2$ × 8 in./264 × 202 mm
HM 941

101

100

102

103

104

103 **Grandparents Anglsperger, reading/Großeltern Anglsperger, lesend**
1928 dated/datiert, red chalk/Rötel,
10 $^3/_4$ × 17 in./270 × 433 mm
HM 489

104 **Massing, Hummel house with market scene/Massing, Marktszene am Hummelhaus**
1928.06, woodcut/Holzschnitt, 2 $^1/_2$ × 3 $^1/_4$ in./66 × 80 mm
HM 623*

105 **Massing, parish church/Massing, Pfarrkirche von Osten**
1928.08, watercolor/Aquarell, 13 $^3/_4$ × 10 in./350 × 257 mm
HM 609

106 **Massing, convent school/Massing, Aufgang zur Klosterschule**
1928.08, watercolor/Aquarell, 13 × 9 $^1/_2$ in./333 × 240 mm
HM 614

105

106

107

110

Kriegerdenkmal

108

107 **Massing, war memorial/Massing, Kriegerdenkmal**
1928.09, watercolor/Aquarell, 10 × 9 $\frac{1}{2}$ in./230 × 322 mm
HM 615

108 **Massing, war memorial/Massing, Kriegerdenkmal**
1928, woodcut/Holzschnitt, 9 × 12 $\frac{3}{4}$ in./110 × 80 mm
HM 659

109 **Massing, Schlossergasse**
1928, pen and ink, crayon/Tusche, Farbstift,
4 $\frac{1}{4}$ × 3 $\frac{1}{4}$ in./205 × 176 mm
HM 605

110 **Massing, Castle Hellsberg/Massing, Schloss Hellsberg**
1928.09, watercolor/Aquarell, 8 × 7 in./255 × 240 mm
HM 620

111 **Massing, house of the Sommerstorfer family/Massing, Sommerstorfer Haus**
1928, pen and ink, crayon/Tusche, Farbstift,
8 $\frac{1}{4}$ × 7 in./208 × 178 mm
HM 601

109

111

112

115

113

116

114

112 **Massing, old smithy/Massing, Schwareiter Schmiedhaus**
1928, pen and ink, crayon/Tusche, Farbstift,
7 ³/₄ × 9 ³/₄ in./195 × 247 mm
HM 607

113 **Anzenberg**
1928.09, pen and ink/Tusche, 6 × 7 in./310 × 232 mm
HM 612

114 **Massing, Brandgasse**
1928, pen and ink/Tusche, 12 ¹/₄ × 9 ¹/₄ in./210 × 165 mm
HM 606

115 **Massing, old smithy/Massing, Schwareiter Schmiedhaus**
1928, pencil/Bleistift, 13 × 9 ¹/₄ in./150 × 175 mm
HM 641

116 **Anzenberg**
1928, pen and ink/Tusche, 8 ¹/₄ × 6 ¹/₂ in./330 × 237 mm
HM 613

117

118

119

120

121

117 **Massing, Brandgasse**
1928, pen and ink/Tusche, 8 $^1/_4$ × 6 $^1/_2$ in./207 × 163 mm
Privat

118 **Massing, Brandgasse**
1928 1.H., woodcut/Holzschnitt, 3 $^3/_4$ × 3 in./96 × 79 mm
HM 657

119 **Massing, house of the Sommerstorfer family/Massing,
Sommersdorfer Haus**
1928, woodcut/Holzschnitt, 3 $^1/_4$ × 2 $^1/_2$ in./80 × 65 mm
HM 624*

120 **Massing, old smithy/Massing, Schwareiter Schmiedhaus**
1928.09, watercolor/Aquarell, 9 $^3/_4$ × 12 in./248 × 307 mm
HM 616

121 **Massing, house of the Hiermann family/Massing, Hiermannhaus**
1928.09, watercolor/Aquarell, 9 $^3/_4$ × 12 $^3/_4$ in./248 × 323 mm
HM 619

122 **Massing, house of the Niederer family/Massing, Niedererhaus**
1928, watercolor/Aquarell, 9 $^3/_4$ × 12 $^3/_4$ in./249 × 324 mm
HM 617

122

123

123 **Portrait of the cobbler Johann Huber/Porträt Johann Huber**
1928.09, red chalk/Rötel, 9 × 7 $^3/_4$ in./230 × 200 mm
HM 643

124 **The cobbler Johann Huber at his work/Schuster Johann Huber arbeitend**
1928.09, red chalk/Rötel, 114 $^1/_4$ × 9 in./290 × 230 mm
HM 645

125 **Margarete, the cobbler's wife/Margarete Huber, Schuhmachersgattin**
1928.09, red chalk/Rötel, 12 $^1/_4$ × 8 $^3/_4$ in./310 × 220 mm
HM 646

126 **Portrait of Anton Graser/Porträt Anton Graser (1849–1929)**
1928, red chalk/Rötel, 11 $^1/_2$ × 9 $^3/_4$ in./290 × 245 mm
HM 647

127 **Portrait of Maria Graser/Porträt Maria Graser (1859–1945)**
1928, red chalk/Rötel, 11 $^1/_2$ × 9 $^3/_4$ in./290 × 245 mm
HM 648

124

126

125

127

128

131

128 **Johann Huber, night watchman/Johann Huber, Nachtwächter**
1928, red chalk/Rötel, 12 $^1/_4$ × 8 $^3/_4$ in./310 × 220 mm
HM 649

129 **Young children (study)/Drei Kleinkinderstudien**
1928, red chalk/Rötel, 7 $^1/_2$ × 5 $^1/_2$ in./190 × 140 mm
HM 49

130 **Head study of a child/Kopfstudie eines Kindes**
1928, red chalk/Rötel, 3 $^1/_2$ × 3 in./88 × 79 mm
HM 47

131 **Little boy, seated/Bub, sitzend**
1928, red chalk/Rötel, 9 $^1/_2$ × 4 $^1/_4$ in./240 × 110 mm
HM 51

132 **Little girl with a ball/Mädchen mit Ball**
1928, red chalk/Rötel, 9 $^1/_2$ × 5 in./240 × 125 mm
HM 52

129

130

132

133

133 Head studies, diverse/Kopfstudien, verschiedene
1928, pencil/Bleistift, 4 $^1/_4$ × 6 in./109 × 150 mm
HM 48

134 Helene with her doll/Helene mit Puppe
1928.10, red chalk/Rötel, 9 $^3/_4$ × 7 $^1/_2$ in./245 × 190 mm
HM 902

135 Massing, convent school/Massing, Klosterschule
1928.10, pen and ink/Tusche, 10 $^1/_2$ × 7 $^1/_2$ in./75 × 115 mm
HM 622

136 Portrait of Helene Anglsperger/Porträt Helene Anglsperger
1928, charcoal/Kohle, 3 × 4 $^1/_2$ in./265 × 190 mm
HM 901

137 Massing, cemetery chapel/Massing, Kirchhof mit Leichenhaus
1928.10, pencil/Bleistift, 5 $^1/_2$ × 8 in./140 × 205 mm
HM 621

134

136

135

137

138

140

139

138 **Massing, Schlossergasse**
1928.12, woodcut/Holzschnitt, 2 $^3/_4$ × 4 $^1/_4$ in./72 × 107 mm
HM 625*

139 **Massing, market square in winter/Massing, Marktplatz im Winter**
1928.12, pencil/Bleistift, 9 $^1/_4$ × 12 $^1/_2$ in./235 × 320 mm
HM 618

140 **Massing parish church in winter/Massing, Pfarrkirche im Winter**
1928.12, woodcut/Holzschnitt, 2 $^3/_4$ × 2 $^1/_4$ in./70 × 56 mm
HM 631

141 **Massing, mill at the bridge/Massing, Bruckmühle**
1928, pen and ink, crayon/Tusche, Farbstift,
8 × 6 $^3/_4$ in./205 × 173 mm
HM 602

141

142

143

144

145

142 **Massing, mill at the bridge/Massing, Bruckmühle**
1928, lithograph/Lithographie, 8 × 5 ¹/₂ in./203 × 141 mm
HM 603

143 **Massing, mill at the bridge/Massing, Bruckmühle**
1928, lithograph/Lithographie, 8 × 5 ¹/₂ in./203 × 141 mm
HM 604

144 **Massing, mill at the bridge/Massing, Bruckmühle**
1928, woodcut/Holzschnitt, 3 ³/₄ × 3 in./97 × 79 mm
HM 658

145 **The dog "Lord" (fragment)/Der Hund »Lord« (Fragment)**
1928, watercolor/Aquarell, cropped/beschnitten
HM 903b

146 **Merry Christmas II/Frohe Weihnacht II**
1928/29, woodcut/Holzschnitt, 2 ³/₄ × 2 ¹/₂ in./68 × 66 mm
HM 661

147 **Bird/Vogel**
1928, pencil/Bleistift, cropped/beschnitten
HM 196b

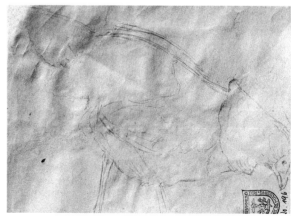

147

146

148

148 **Flowers in a bowl/Blumen in Kugelvase**
1928/29, graphite/Graphit, 14 $^1/_2$ × 12 $^1/_4$ in./370 × 310 mm
HM 256

149 **Anemones and daisies/Anemonen und Margeriten**
1928/29, watercolor/Aquarell, cropped/beschnitten
HM 893a

150 **Daisies and primroses with vessels/Margeriten und Schlüsselblumen mit Krügen**
1928/29, watercolor/Aquarell, 12 $^3/_4$ × 19 in./325 × 483 mm
HM 325a

151 **Spring flowers/Frühlingsblumen**
1928/29, watercolor/Aquarell, cropped/beschnitten
HM 893b

149

151

150

152

153

154

152 **Vase of flowers/Blumen in der Vase**
1928/29, watercolor/Aquarell, 19 × 13 in./480 × 330 mm
HM 335a

153 **White tulips in a flowerpot/Weiße Tulpen in Blumentopf**
1928/29, watercolor/Aquarell, 22 $^3/_4$ × 16 $^3/_4$ in./580 × 425 mm
HM 326

154 **Tulips in a curved vase/Tulpen in bauchiger Vase**
1928/36, watercolor/Aquarell, 15 $^1/_4$ × 20 $^1/_2$ in./385 × 523 mm
KS E

155 **Tulips in a tall vase/Tulpen in schlanker Vase**
1928/36, watercolor/Aquarell, 23 $^1/_2$ × 17 $^1/_4$ in./590 × 440 mm
KS F

156 **Lilies in a flowerpot/Lilien in Topf**
1928/29, watercolor/Aquarell, 21 $^1/_2$ × 15 $^1/_2$ in./545 × 395 mm
HM 322

157 **Lilies in a flowerpot/Lilien in Topf**
1928/29, watercolor/Aquarell, 19 × 16 in./480 × 404 mm
HM 483

155

156

157

158

160

159

161

158 **Blossoms in glass vase (fragment)/Blüten im Glas (Fragment)**
1928/29, watercolor/Aquarell, cropped/beschnitten
HM 844b

159 **Potplant/Blumenstock ohne Blüte**
1928/29, watercolor/Aquarell, 13 $^1/_2$ × 11 $^1/_4$ in./344 × 287 mm
HM 844a

160 **Geranium and gloxinia/Geranie und Gloxinie**
1928/29, watercolor/Aquarell, 20 $^3/_4$ × 15 $^1/_4$ in./530 × 390 mm
HM 323

161 **Anemones in glass vase/Anemonen in bauchiger Glasvase**
1928/29, watercolor/Aquarell, 16 $^1/_4$ × 12 in./413 × 306 mm
HM 845a

162

164

163

165

162 **Begonia/Begonie**
1928/29, watercolor/Aquarell, 12 $^1/_2$ × 12 $^3/_4$ in./320 × 325 mm
HM 502b

163 **Young girl, seated/Mädchen, sitzend**
1928/29, watercolor, pencil/Aquarell, Bleistift,
16 $^1/_2$ × 9 $^1/_2$ in./420 × 243 mm
HM 237

164 **Begonia/Begonie**
1928/29, watercolor/Aquarell, 14 $^1/_2$ × 12 $^1/_2$ in./371 × 320 mm
HM 502a

165 **Portrait of a boy/Porträt eines Knaben**
1928/29, watercolor/Aquarell, 7 $^3/_4$ × 6 $^1/_4$ in./200 × 160 mm
HM 495

166

169

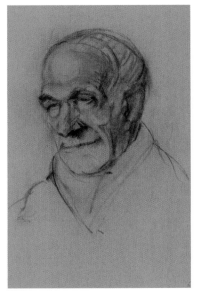

167

168

170

166 **Portrait of a woman/Porträt einer Frau**
1928/29, charcoal/Kohle, 9 $^3/_4$ × 7 $^1/_4$ in./250 × 184 mm
HM 140

167 **Portrait of a man/Porträt eines Mannes**
1928/29, charcoal/Kohle, 14 $^1/_2$ × 11 $^3/_4$ in./370 × 300 mm
HM 228

168 **Portrait of a woman/Porträt einer Frau**
1928/29, charcoal/Kohle, 11 $^3/_4$ × 9 $^3/_4$ in./300 × 250 mm
HM 464

169 **Portrait of a man/Porträt eines Mannes**
1928/29, charcoal/Kohle, 14 $^1/_4$ × 11 $^1/_2$ in./360 × 290 mm
HM 225

170 **Portrait of a young woman/Porträt einer jungen Frau**
1928/29, charcoal/Kohle, 11 $^3/_4$ × 10 $^1/_2$ in./300 × 264 mm
HM 134

171

175

172

173

176

174

171 **Massing, view from the hill/Massing vom Kirchberg aus**
1928/29, watercolor/Aquarell, 10 $^1/_2$ × 19 $^1/_2$ in./265 × 494 mm
HM 608

172 **Massing, parish church, north view/Massing, Pfarrkirche von Norden**
1928/29, watercolor/Aquarell, cropped/beschnitten
HM 55b

173 **Still life with green bottle/Stillleben mit grüner Flasche**
1928/30, watercolor/Aquarell, 15 × 20 $^1/_2$1 in./380 × 522 mm
HM 260

174 **Still life with fruit and vessels/Stillleben mit Obst und Geschirr**
1928/30, watercolor/Aquarell, 10 $^1/_2$ × 18 in./265 × 460 mm
HM 479a

175 **Bavarian graveyard/Kirchhof in Oberbayern**
1928/29, watercolor/Aquarell, 16 × 11 $^1/_2$ in./405 × 295 mm
HM 267

176 **Bavarian country graveyard/Alte Gräber in Oberbayern**
1928/29, watercolor/Aquarell, 16 $^1/_2$ × 11 $^3/_4$ in./417 × 297 mm
HM 934

177

179

177 **Over the roofs/Über den Dächern**
1928/30, watercolor/Aquarell, 9 $^1/_2$ × 15 $^3/_4$ in./235 × 400 mm
HM 352

178 **Munich, bird's-eye view/Münchener Dächer**
1928/30, watercolor/Aquarell, 23 $^1/_4$ × 17 $^1/_2$ in./592 × 445 mm
HM 852

179 **Burghausen**
1928/30, watercolor/Aquarell, 11 $^3/_4$ × 16 $^1/_4$ in./298 × 414 mm
HM 478

180 **Head of a tiger/Tigerkopf**
1928/29, watercolor/Aquarell, 22 $^1/_4$ × 16 $^1/_4$ in./563 × 411 mm
HM 851

178

180

181

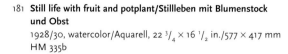

181 **Still life with fruit and potplant/Stillleben mit Blumenstock und Obst**
1928/30, watercolor/Aquarell, 22 $\frac{3}{4}$ × 16 $\frac{1}{2}$ in./577 × 417 mm
HM 335b

182 **Flowerpiece with two flasks/Blumenstillleben mit zwei Flaschen**
1928/30, watercolor/Aquarell, 20 $\frac{3}{4}$ × 14 $\frac{1}{2}$ in./529 × 371 mm
HM 889

183 **Blue hydrangeas/Blaue Hortensien**
1928/30, watercolor/Aquarell, 17 × 23 in./432 × 584 mm
HM 336b

184 **Sunflowers in a glass/Sonnenblumen im Glas**
1928/30, watercolor/Aquarell, 15 $\frac{3}{4}$ × 11 in./399 × 282 mm
HM 843b

185 **Wild flowers in brown vase/Wiesenblumen in brauner Vase**
1928/30, watercolor/Aquarell, 20 $\frac{1}{2}$ × 15 $\frac{1}{4}$ in./520 × 390 mm
HM 330

182

184

183

185

186

188

187

189

186 **Wild flowers/Wiesenblumenstrauß**
1928/30, watercolor/Aquarell, 21 $^3/_4$ × 15 $^1/_4$ in./550 × 390 mm
HM 331

187 **Red cineraria I/Rote Cinerarie I**
1928/30, watercolor/Aquarell, 17 $^1/_4$ × 10 $^1/_4$ in./439 × 260 mm
HM 933a

188 **Anemones and primulas in tall vase/Anemonen und Primeln in
hoher Glasvase**
1928/30, watercolor/Aquarell, 21 $^1/_4$ × 15 $^1/_4$ in./540 × 390 mm
HM 324

189 **Red cineraria II/Rote Cinerarie II**
1928/30, watercolor/Aquarell, 17 $^1/_4$ × 10 $^1/_4$ in./439 × 260 mm
HM 933b

190

191

192

190 **Daffodils and anemones/Osterglocken und Anemonen**
1928/30, watercolor/Aquarell, measurements unknown/Maß
unbekannt
HM 936

191 **Poinsettia/Weihnachtsstern**
1928/30, watercolor/Aquarell, 19 $^1/_2$× 13 $^3/_4$ in./498 × 348 mm
HM 838a

192 **Poinsettia/Weihnachtsstern**
1928/30, watercolor/Aquarell, 19 $^1/_2$ × 13 $^3/_4$ in./498 × 348 mm
HM 838b

193 **Autumn bouquet/Herbststrauß**
1928/30, watercolor/Aquarell, 16 × 11 $^1/_2$ in./405 × 290 mm
HM 857

194 **Certificate, Simbach school 1929/Absolvia Simbach 1929**
1929, woodcut/Holzschnitt, 5 $^3/_4$ × 4 in./147 × 104 mm
HM 446*

193

194

195

198

196

195 **Portrait of Jakob Huber from the Gangerfinger property/Porträt Jakob Huber – Gangerfinger Vater**
1929, watercolor/Aquarell, 13 $^3/_4$ × 9 $^1/_2$ in./352 × 244 mm
HM 650

196 **Portrait of Viktoria Hummel/Porträt Viktoria Hummel**
1929.04, charcoal/Kohle, 11 × 10 $^1/_4$ in./280 × 260 mm
HM 434

197 **Portrait of Adolf Hummel/Porträt Adolf Hummel**
1929.03, charcoal/Kohle, 11 × 10 $^1/_4$ in./280 × 260 mm
HM 435

198 **The cobbler Johann Huber at his work/Schuster Johann Huber arbeitend**
1929.03, watercolor/Aquarell, 14 × 9 $^3/_4$ in./353 × 250 mm
HM 644

199 **Portrait of a man/Porträt eines Mannes**
1929, charcoal/Kohle, 10 $^1/_2$ × 7 $^3/_4$ in./270 × 200 mm
HM 151

197

199

200

200 Portrait of Georg Anglsperger/Porträt Georg Anglsperger
1929, charcoal/Kohle, 12 $^1/_4$ × 8 $^3/_4$ in./313 × 225 mm
HM 527

201 Portrait of a man with beard/Porträt eines Mannes mit Bart
1929, charcoal/Kohle, 10 × 7 $^1/_4$ in./255 × 183 mm
HM 159

202 Portrait of a man with beard/Porträt eines Mannes mit Bart
1929, charcoal/Kohle, 11 $^3/_4$ × 8 in./297 × 204 mm
HM 906

203 Portrait of a man/Porträt eines Mannes
1929, charcoal/Kohle, 17 × 10 $^3/_4$ in./430 × 270 mm
HM 226

204 Portrait of a man/Porträt eines Mannes
1929, charcoal/Kohle, 13 $^1/_2$ × 9 $^3/_4$ in./346 × 247 mm
HM 928

205 Head study of a woman (fragment)
Kopfstudie einer Frau (Fragment)
1929, charcoal/Kohle, cropped/beschnitten
HM 145b

201

203

202

204

205

206

208

209

207

206 **Crucified Christ/Christus am Kreuz**
1929, watercolor/Aquarell, 20 × 11 ¹/₂ in./510 × 290 mm
HM 860

207 **Maria Laach Madonna/Maria mit Kind**
(nach einem Vorbild aus Maria Laach)
1929, oil/Öl, 48 ¹/₂ × 38 in./1225 × 963 mm
Privat

208 **Crucified Christ/Christus am Kreuz**
1929, watercolor/Aquarell, 16 ¹/₂ × 13 ¹/₂ in./419 × 345 mm
HM 859

209 **Crucified Christ/Christus am Kreuz**
1929, woodcut/Holzschnitt, 3 × 2 ¹/₄ in./74 × 58 mm
HM 632

210

213

211

210 **Portrait of Maxl Neubauer/Porträt Maxl Neubauer**
1929, charcoal/Kohle, 12 $^1/_2$ × 7 $^1/_4$ in./315 × 184 mm
Privat

211 **Berta Hummel, self-portrait/Selbstporträt Berta Hummel**
1929, red chalk/Rötel, 10 × 7 $^1/_4$ in./252 × 187 mm
HM 514

212 **Old man with stooped back/Alter Mann, gebückt sitzend**
1929, charcoal/Kohle, 9 $^1/_2$ × 79,53 in./240 × 202 mm
HM 201

213 **Peasant woman with head-scarf/Bäuerin mit Kopftuch**
1929, watercolor/Aquarell, 10 $^3/_4$ × 18 $^1/_2$ in./272 × 468 mm
HM 479b

214 **Young woman, motion study/Frau, halb sitzend**
1929, charcoal, Pittchalk/Kohle, Pittkreide,
15 $^3/_4$ × 7 $^1/_4$ in./400 × 187 mm
HM 241

212

214

215

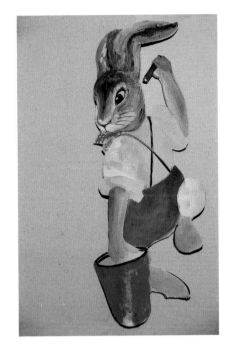

217

216

218

215-218 **Window decorations, Easter 1929/Schaufensterdekoration**
für Ostern 1929
HM 453/1-4

215 **Mother Rabbit with children/Hasenmutter mit zwei Kindern**
1929, watercolor/Wasserfarbe, 23 × 19 in./585 × 480 mm
HM 453/1

216 **Father Rabbit house-painting/Hasenvater auf der Leiter, malend**
1929, watercolor/Wasserfarbe, 19 $\frac{1}{2}$ × 9 $\frac{1}{2}$ in./495 × 240 mm
HM 453/2

217 **Young Rabbit on ladder/Hasenjunge auf der Leiter**
1929, watercolor/Wasserfarbe, 18 $\frac{1}{4}$ × 7 $\frac{1}{2}$ in./465 × 190 mm
HM 453/3

218 **Young Rabbit at window/Hasenjunge am Fenster**
1929, watercolor/Wasserfarbe, 12 $\frac{1}{2}$ × 6 $\frac{1}{4}$ in./315 × 160 mm
HM 453/4

219-226 Window decorations, Christmas 1929
Schaufensterdekoration für Weihnachten 1929
HM 448/1-7

223

219

220

219 Christ Child with two angels/Christkind mit zwei Engeln
1929, watercolor/Wasserfarbe, 4 $\frac{1}{2}$ × 5 $\frac{1}{2}$ in./117 × 142 mm
HM 448/1

220 Two angels with parcels/Zwei Engel mit Paketen
1929, watercolor/Wasserfarbe, 4 × 3 in./100 × 76 mm
HM 448/2

221 Two angels with wind instruments/Zwei Engel mit Blasinstrument
1929, watercolor/Wasserfarbe, 4 × 3 in./100 × 78 mm
HM 448/3

222 Five angels with stringed instruments/Fünf Engel mit Streichinstrument
1929, watercolor/Wasserfarbe, 2 $\frac{3}{4}$ × 3 $\frac{1}{4}$ in./68 × 86 mm
HM 448/4

223 Two angels with harps/Zwei Engel mit Harfe
1929, watercolor/Wasserfarbe, 2 $\frac{1}{4}$ × 2 $\frac{3}{4}$ in./60 × 70 mm
HM 448/5

224 Six singing angels with music sheets/Sechs singende Engel mit Notenblatt
1929, watercolor/Wasserfarbe, 3 $\frac{1}{4}$ × 1 $\frac{1}{3}$ in./86 × 47 mm
HM 448/6

221

222

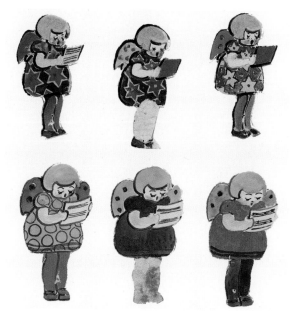

224

225

226

227

228

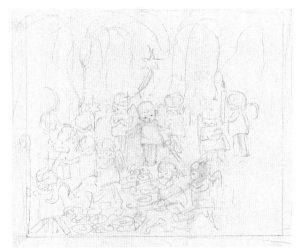

229

225 **Children on sled/Kinder auf dem Schlitten**
1929, watercolor/Wasserfarbe, 10 ³/₄ × 9 ¹/₄ in./273 × 237 mm
HM 448/7

226 **Two angels with Christmas tree/Zwei Engel mit Christbaum**
1929, watercolor, pencil/Wasserfarbe, Bleistift,
7 ¹/₄ × 4 ¹/₂ in./185 × 115 mm
HM 449

227 **New Year greetings 1930: Angel with bell/Neujahrsgrußkarte 1930: Engel mit Glocke**
1929, pencil/Bleistift, 3 ¹/₂ × 2 ¹/₄ in./90 × 55 mm
HM 66

228 **Christmas crib/Christkind zwischen Ochs und Esel**
1929, pencil/Bleistift, 2 ¹/₄ × 2 ¹/₄ in./55 × 55 mm
HM 77

229 **Christ Child with angels/Christkind mit Engelschar**
1929, pencil/Bleistift, 5 ¹/₄ × 6 ¹/₄ in./132 × 156 mm
HM 119

230

232

231

233

234

230 **Merry Christmas I (alternative state)/Frohe Weihnacht I (Zustandsdruck)**
1929, woodcut/Holzschnitt, 2 $^3/_4$ × 2 $^1/_4$ in./71 × 57 mm
HM 660A

231 **Merry Christmas I/Frohe Weihnacht I**
1929 dated/datiert, woodcut/Holzschnitt,
2 $^1/_4$ × 2 $^1/_4$ in./60 × 57 mm
HM 660D✳

232 **Christmas crib/Weihnachtskrippe**
1929, colored woodcut/Holzschnitt, kolor.,
3 $^1/_4$ × 2 $^1/_2$ in./85 × 62 mm
HM 629A✳

233 **Christ Child riding toy donkey/Christkind, reitend auf Spielzeug-Esel**
1929, pencil/Bleistift, 1 $^1/_2$ × 2 $^3/_4$ in./40 × 70 mm
HM 74

234 **Christ Child riding toy donkey/Christkind, reitend auf Spielzeug-Esel**
1929, pencil/Bleistift, 1 $^1/_2$ × 2 $^3/_4$ in./40 × 70 mm
HM 75

235

238

236

239

237

235 **Christ Child riding toy donkey/Christkind, reitend auf Spielzeug-Esel**
1929, etching/Radierung, 1 $^1/_2$ × 2 $^3/_4$ in./40 × 70 mm
HM 76A

236 **Christ Child riding toy donkey/Christkind, reitend auf Spielzeug-Esel**
1929, etching/Radierung, 1 $^3/_4$ × 2 $^3/_4$ in./40 × 70 mm
HM 76B

237 **City pastimes/Kinder in der Stadt**
1929, pencil/Bleistift, 4 $^1/_4$ × 2 $^1/_4$ in./105 × 60 mm
HM 63

238 **Christ Child on donkey with angels/Christkind auf Esel mit Engeln**
1929 dated/datiert, lithograph/Lithographie,
7 $^3/_4$ × 7 $^3/_4$ in./200 × 195 mm
HM 172

239 **New Year zest/Neujahrsstimmung**
1929, pencil/Bleistift, 4 $^1/_4$ × 2 $^1/_4$ in./105 × 60 mm
HM 62

240

243

241

240 **New Year music/Neujahrsmusikanten**
1929, pencil/Bleistift, 4 × 2 $^1/_4$ in./100 × 55 mm
HM 65

241 **Hummel trademark/Hummel Firmenzeichen**
1929, watercolor/Wasserfarbe, 6 $^3/_4$ × 8 $^1/_4$ in./170 × 207 mm
HM 590

242 **Massing, Berta Hummel Street/Massing, Berta-Hummel-Straße**
1929.03, watercolor/Aquarell, 13 $^3/_4$ × 11 $^1/_2$ in./351 × 290 mm
HM 640

243 **Topsy-turvy/Betrunkenen-Perspektive**
1929, pencil/Bleistift, 4 × 2 $^1/_4$ in./99 × 54 mm
HM 846

244 **Massing, Berta Hummel Street/Massing, Berta-Hummel-Straße**
1929.04, watercolor/Aquarell, 12 $^1/_4$ × 9 in./310 × 230 mm
HM 652

242

244

245

248

246

249

247

245 **Massing, market square in spring/Massing, Marktplatz im Frühjahr**
1929.04, watercolor/Aquarell, 16 $^1/_2$ × 9 $^1/_2$ in./416 × 242 mm
HM 651

246 **Massing, parish church with graveyard/Massing, Pfarrkirche mit Friedhof**
1929.07, watercolor/Aquarell, 9 × 12 $^1/_2$ in./230 × 320 mm
HM 653

247 **View of Massing and Anzenberg/Blick auf Massing und Anzenberg**
1929.07, watercolor/Aquarell, 9 × 12 $^3/_4$ in./230 × 324 mm
HM 656

248 **View towards Moosvogl/Blick auf Moosvogl**
1929.07, watercolor/Aquarell, 13 × 10 in./328 × 255 mm
HM 655

249 **View of the Rott valley/Rottal vom Kalvarienberg aus**
1929.07, watercolor/Aquarell, 10 $^1/_4$ × 12 $^1/_2$ in./260 × 320 mm
HM 654

250

250 **Market scene/Marktszene**
1929, pencil/Bleistift, 7 × 6 ¹/₂ in./177 × 167 mm
HM 46

251 **Massing, the wax marktet/Massing, Wachsmarkt**
1929, oil/Öl, 17 ¹/₄ × 13 in./441 × 330 mm
HM 486

252 **Corpus Christi Procession in Massing/Fronleichnamsprozession in Massing**
1929, oil/Öl, 13 × 17 ¹/₄ in./332 × 438 mm
HM 498

253 **Massing, parish church, view from the Rott valley/Massing, Pfarrkirche von der Rott aus**
1929, oil/Öl, 13 ¹/₄ × 17 in./335 × 430 mm
HM 485

251

253

252

254

257

255

256

258

254 **Massing Fire-brigade, 60th-anniversary card (design)/60jähriges Feuerwehrjubiläum Massing (Entwurf)**
1929, pencil/Bleistift, 3 $^1/_2$ × 4 $^3/_4$ in./92 × 120 mm
HM 642A

255 **Munich, in the Au/München, in der Au**
1929, watercolor/Aquarell, 16 × 10 $^3/_4$ in./405 × 275 mm
HM 863a

256 **Munich, Ludwigstrasse, view towards the Siegestor/München, Ludwigstraße zum Siegestor**
1929 dated/datiert, watercolor/Aquarell,
18 $^1/_4$ × 23 $^3/_4$ in./463 × 605 mm
HM 942

257 **Massing Fire-brigade, 60th-anniversary card/60jähriges Feuerwehrjubiläum Massing**
1929, woodcut/Holzschnitt, 4 $^1/_4$ × 5 $^3/_4$ in./110 × 145 mm
HM 642B

258 **Street with column/Straßenansicht mit Bildsäule**
1929/30, watercolor/Aquarell, 16 $^1/_2$ × 16 $^1/_4$ in./422 × 412 mm
Privat

259

260

262

261

263

264

267

265

268

266

264 **Alpine forest/Gebirgslandschaft mit Wald**
1929/30, watercolor/Aquarell, 21 $^3/_4$ × 16 in./555 × 405 mm
HM 528

265 **Alpine landscape/Gebirgslandschaft**
1929/30, watercolor/Aquarell, 11 $^1/_2$ × 16 $^1/_4$ in./295 × 412 mm
HM 866

266 **Alpine landscape/Gebirgslandschaft**
1929/30, watercolor/Aquarell, 11 $^1/_4$ × 15 $^3/_4$ in./285 × 400 mm
HM 266

267 **Chiemsee landscape/Am Chiemsee**
1929/30, watercolor/Aquarell, 15 $^1/_2$ × 12 $^1/_4$ in./395 × 310 mm
HM 264

268 **By the lake/Landschaft mit See**
1929/30, watercolor/Aquarell, 17 $^1/_4$ × 23 in./435 × 583 mm
HM 940

269

272

270

269 **Over the roofs of Salzburg/Salzburg, Blick auf den Dom**
1929/30, watercolor/Aquarell, 16 $^1/_4$ × 11 $^1/_2$ in./410 × 291 mm
HM 861

270 **Salzburg, Collegiate Church/Salzburg, Blick auf die Kollegienkirche**
1929/30, watercolor/Aquarell, 16 $^1/_4$ × 11 $^1/_2$ in./410 × 291 mm
HM 862

271 **Salzburg environs/Salzburger Land**
1929/30, watercolor/Aquarell, 16 $^1/_4$ × 11 $^3/_4$ in./415 × 299 mm
HM 865

272 **Salzburg, the old fort/Salzburger Festung**
1929/30, watercolor/Aquarell, 16 $^1/_4$ × 11 $^3/_4$ in./415 × 299 mm
HM 926

273 **View of Salzburg/Salzburg**
1929/30, watercolor/Aquarell, 15 $^3/_4$ × 21 $^1/_2$ in./400 × 545 mm
HM 353

271

273

274

275

277

276

274 **Romanesque cloister/Romanischer Kreuzgang**
1929/30, watercolor/Aquarell, 10 $^3/_4$ × 15 $^3/_4$ in./271 × 398 mm
HM 529

275 **Market in Munich/München, Viktualienmarkt**
1929/30, watercolor/Aquarell, 10 × 13 $^3/_4$ in./251 × 348 mm
HM 265

276 **Town well/Stadtbrunnen**
1929/36, graphite/Graphit, 12 $^1/_4$ × 9 $^1/_4$ in./314 × 234 mm
HM 263

277 **Gothic cloister/Gotischer Kreuzgang**
1929/30, watercolor/Aquarell, 22 $^3/_4$ × 17 in./580 × 430 mm
HM 356

278

280

279

278 **Bregenz, view from Lindau/Bregenz von Lindau aus**
1929/36, pencil/Bleistift, 10 $^3/_4$ × 13 $^3/_4$ in./270 × 350 mm
HM 566,1

279 **Lake Constance/Bodensee mit Halbinsel Lindau**
1929/36, pencil/Bleistift, 4 $^1/_4$ × 9 in./110 × 230 mm
HM 58

280 **Woods near Lindau/Waldlandschaft bei Lindau**
1929/36, graphite/Graphit, 8 $^3/_4$ × 11 $^3/_4$ in./225 × 296 mm
HM 204

281 **Fir-tree/Baumstudie mit Föhre**
1929/30, pencil/Bleistift, 15 $^3/_4$ × 9 in./400 × 228 mm
HM 261

282 **Fir-trees/Föhren**
1929/30, watercolor/Aquarell, 21 $^1/_4$ × 15 $^1/_4$ in./538 × 390 mm
HM 896

283 **Fir-woods/Föhrenwald**
1929/30, watercolor/Aquarell, 23 $^1/_4$ × 17 $^1/_2$ in./593 × 442 mm
HM 494

281

282

283

284

285

286

287

288

289

284 **In the forest/Waldstudie**
1929/30, watercolor/Aquarell, 16 ¹/₄ × 11 ³/₄ in./414 × 297 mm
KS G

285 **Sproce-Tree/Waldstudie mit Fichte**
1929/30, watercolor/Aquarell, 23 ¹/₂ × 17 ¹/₂ in./595 × 444 mm
HM 285 privat

286 **Birch forest/Birkenwald**
1929/30, watercolor/Aquarell, 19 ¹/₂ × 13 ³/₄ in./496 × 351 mm
HM 858a

287 **Alpine landscape with fir-trees/Gebirgslandschaft mit Tannen**
1929/30, watercolor/Aquarell, 13 × 18 ³/₄ in./329 × 477 mm
HM 858b

288 **Lakeside path/Straße am See**
1929/30, watercolor/Aquarell, 13 ¹/₂ × 19 in./341 × 485 mm
HM 939

289 **Chiemsee steamer/Dampfer auf dem Chiemsee**
1929/30, watercolor/Aquarell, 13 ³/₄ × 18 ¹/₄ in./347 × 465 mm
HM 869

290

291

292

293

290 **Living room with crucifix/Stube mit Herrgotts-Winkel**
1929/30, watercolor/Aquarell, 13 $^3/_4$ × 18 in./352 × 457 mm
HM 943

291 **Biedermeier interior/Biedermeier-Zimmer**
1929/30, watercolor/Aquarell, 18 $^1/_4$ × 14 $^1/_4$ in./463 × 361 mm
HM 867

292 **Church steps/Kirchenaufgang mit Figur**
1929/30, watercolor/Aquarell, 19 × 12 $^1/_4$ in./481 × 308 mm
HM 824a

293 **Sculpture by arched doorway/Figurengruppe neben Bogeneingang**
1929/30, watercolor/Aquarell, 18 $^1/_2$ × 11 $^1/_4$ in./473 × 286 mm
HM 824b

294

297

295

294 **Statue between candles/Standbild zwischen zwei Kerzen**
1929/30, watercolor/Aquarell, 12 $^3/_4$ × 8 $^1/_4$ in./322 × 213 mm
HM 868

295 **Geraniums and gloxinias/Geranie und Gloxinie**
1929 dated/datiert, watercolor/Aquarell,
20 $^3/_4$ × 15 $^1/_4$ in./530 × 390 mm
HM 329

296 **Flower bench/Blumenfenster**
1929/30, watercolor/Aquarell, 20 $^1/_2$ × 15 $^3/_4$ in./520 × 385 mm
HM 328

297 **Blue cineraria in flowerpot/Blaue Cinerarie in Blumentopf**
1929/30, watercolor/Aquarell, 21 $^1/_2$ × 15 $^3/_4$ in./547 × 401 mm
HM 891

298 **Bleeding heart (Dicentra)/Tränendes Herz (Dicentra)**
1929/30, watercolor/Aquarell, 16 × 10 $^3/_4$ in./405 × 275 mm
HM 863b

296

298

299

302

300

299 **Lilies on blue background/Zwei Lilien vor blauem Grund**
1929/30, watercolor/Aquarell, 17 $\frac{1}{4}$ × 13 in./440 × 330 mm
HM 864b

300 **Daffodils and freesias/Osterglocken und Freesien**
1929/30, watercolor/Aquarell, 18 $\frac{3}{4}$ × 12 $\frac{1}{2}$ in./475 × 320 mm
HM 890b

301 **Flowers in brown vase/Blumen in rotbrauner Vase**
1929/30, watercolor/Aquarell, 14 $\frac{1}{4}$ × 20 in./360 × 505 mm
HM 336a

302 **Daisies in white jug/Margeriten in hellem Krug**
1929/30, watercolor/Aquarell, 20 $\frac{1}{2}$ × 15 in./520 × 380 mm
HM 327a

301

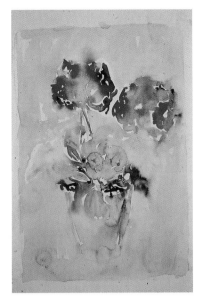

303

306

304

307

305

303 **Red primula (fragment)/Rote Primeln in Topf (Fragment)**
1929/30, watercolor/Aquarell, 20 $^1/_2$ × 15 in./520 × 380 mm
HM 327b

304 **Ranunculae/Ranunkeln**
1929/30, watercolor/Aquarell, 16 × 20 in./405 × 505 mm
HM 332

305 **Red dahlias/Rote Dahlien**
1929/30, watercolor/Aquarell, 16 $^1/_4$ × 11 $^3/_4$ in./415 × 298 mm
HM 532

306 **Flowers in striped jug/Blumen in blauweißem Krug**
1929/30, watercolor/Aquarell, 21 $^1/_4$ × 15 $^1/_2$ in./540 × 395 mm
HM 334

307 **Flowers and thistles/Bunte Blumen mit Disteln**
1929/30, watercolor/Aquarell, cropped/beschnitten
HM 221b

308

311

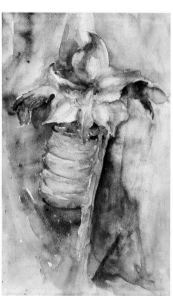

309

312

310

308 **Epiphyllum**
1929/30, watercolor/Aquarell, 19 × 12 ¹/₂ in./480 × 320 mm
HM 894

309 **Amaryllis with Chinese lantern/Amaryllis mit Lampion**
1929/30, watercolor/Aquarell, 20 × 12 ¹/₄ in./510 × 314 mm
HM 932

310 **Red dahlia (fragment)/Rote Dahlie (Fragment)**
1929/30, watercolor/Aquarell
KS H

311 **Summer flowers/Sommerblumen in dunkler Vase**
1929/30, watercolor/Aquarell, 20 ¹/₂ × 14 ³/₄ in./520 × 373 mm
HM 821

312 **Chrysanthemum/Chrysantheme**
1929/30, watercolor/Aquarell, 20 × 13 ¹/₂ in./510 × 345 mm
HM 333

313

314

316

315

317

313 **Red cineraria III/Rote Cinerarie III**
1929/30, watercolor/Aquarell, 18 $^3/_4$ × 12 $^1/_2$ in./475 × 320 mm
HM 890a

314 **Campanula in vase/Glockenblumen im Krug**
1929/30, watercolor/Aquarell, 20 $^1/_4$ × 14 $^3/_4$ in./518 × 375 mm
HM 892

315 **Crucifix with flowers/Kruzifix mit Blüten**
1929/30, watercolor/Aquarell, 21 $^1/_4$ × 13 $^3/_4$ in./537 × 348 mm
HM 839

316 **Crucifix with books and candle/Kruzifix mit Kerze und Büchern**
1929/30, watercolor/Aquarell, 20 $^3/_4$ × 14 in./525 × 353 mm
HM 870a

317 **Crucifix with candle/Kruzifix mit Kerze**
1929/30, watercolor/Aquarell, 15 $^3/_4$ × 11 in./399 × 282 mm
HM 843a

318

318 **The dog "Lord"/Der Hund »Lord«**
1929/30, watercolor/Aquarell, 11 $\frac{1}{2}$ × 10 $\frac{1}{2}$ in./293 × 268 mm
HM 209

319 **The dog "Lord"/Der Hund »Lord«**
1929/30, watercolor/Aquarell, 13 $\frac{1}{2}$ × 13 $\frac{1}{2}$ in./340 × 340 mm
HM 210

320 **Portrait of a woman/Porträt einer Frau**
1929/30, charcoal, Pittchalk/Kohle, Pittkreide,
10 $\frac{3}{4}$ × 7 $\frac{3}{4}$ in./270 × 195 mm
HM 139

321 **Study of a man with hat/Kopfstudie eines Mannes mit Hut**
1929/30, watercolor/Aquarell, 20 $\frac{3}{4}$ × 14 in./525 × 353 mm
HM 870b

322 **Young woman, figure study/Frau, stehend**
1929/30, charcoal, Pittchalk/Kohle, Pittkreide,
15 $\frac{1}{4}$ × 8 in./390 × 204 mm
HM 240

319

321

320

322

323

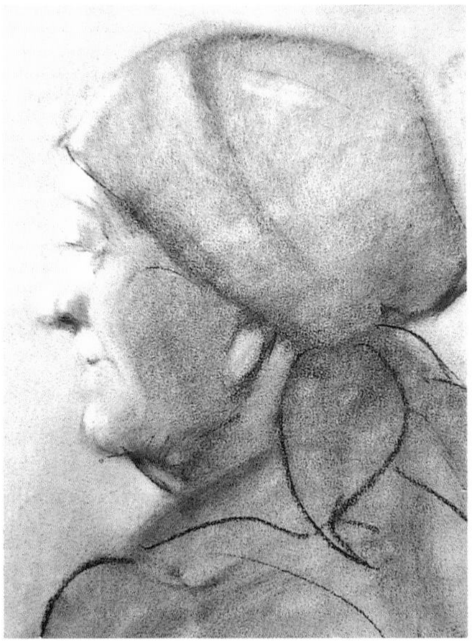

326

324

327

325

323 **Portrait of a peasant woman/Porträt einer Bäuerin**
1929/30, charcoal/Kohle, 10 1/4 × 7 1/2 in./260 × 188 mm
HM 145a

324 **Peasant woman, seated/Bäuerin mit Kopftuch, sitzend**
1929/30, charcoal/Kohle, 9 3/4 × 8 1/2 in./245 × 218 mm
HM 197

325 **Bearded man, seated/Bärtiger Mann, sitzend**
1929/30, charcoal/Kohle, 10 3/4 × 7 in./270 × 180 mm
HM 882

326 **Portrait of a peasant woman/Porträt einer Bäuerin**
1929/30, charcoal/Kohle, 9 3/4 × 8 1/2 in./277 × 209 mm
HM 907

327 **Peasant woman, reading/Lesende Bäuerin mit Kopftuch**
1929/30, Pittchalk, charcoal/Pittkreide, Kohle,
11 1/2 × 6 3/4 in./292 × 173 mm
HM 198

328

331

329

332

330

328 **Portrait of a peasant woman/Porträt einer Bäuerin**
1929/30, charcoal/Kohle, 10 $^3/_4$ × 7 $^1/_2$ in./270 × 188 mm
HM 146

329 **Portrait of a peasant woman/Porträt einer Bäuerin**
1929/30, watercolor/Aquarell, 15 $^3/_4$ × 12 $^1/_4$ in./403 × 310 mm
HM 840a

330 **Head study of a woman (fragment)/**
Kopfstudie einer Frau (Fragment)
1929/30, watercolor/Aquarell, cropped/beschnitten
HM 142b

331 **Portrait of a peasant woman/Porträt einer Bäuerin**
1929/30, charcoal/Kohle, 9 $^3/_4$ × 7 in./249 × 176 mm
HM 826

332 **Portrait of a peasant woman/Porträt einer Bäuerin**
1929/30, watercolor/Aquarell, 15 $^3/_4$ × 12 $^1/_4$ in./403 × 310 mm
HM 840b

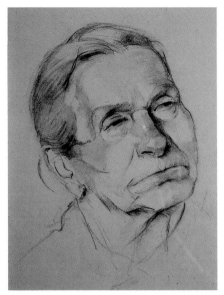

333

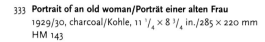

333 Portrait of an old woman/Porträt einer alten Frau
1929/30, charcoal/Kohle, 11 $^1/_4$ × 8 $^3/_4$ in./285 × 220 mm
HM 143

334 Lady in blue/Dame in Blau
1929/30, watercolor, pencil/Aquarell, Bleistift,
19 $^3/_4$ × 11 $^3/_4$ in./500 × 300 mm
HM 243

335 Portrait of a young woman (cf. HM 243)/Porträt einer jungen Frau (vgl. HM 243)
1929/30, charcoal/Kohle, 11 $^1/_2$ × 9 $^1/_4$ in./290 × 235 mm
HM 137

336 Portrait of a man/Porträt eines Mannes
1929/30, charcoal/Kohle, 10 $^3/_4$ × 7 $^1/_2$ in./270 × 188 mm
HM 150

334

335

336

337

340

338

341

339

337 **Portrait of a boy/Porträt eines Knaben**
1929/30, watercolor/Aquarell, 16 × 10 ¹/₂ in./405 × 265 mm
HM 214

338 **Portrait of a young woman with head-scarf/Porträt einer jungen Frau mit Kopftuch**
1929/30, watercolor/Aquarell, 15 ³/₄ × 11 ¹/₂ in./400 × 290 mm
HM 215a

339 **Portrait of a young woman with head-scarf/Porträt einer jungen Frau mit Kopftuch**
1929/30, watercolor/Aquarell, 19 ¹/₄ × 10 ³/₄ in./490 × 270 mm
HM 215b

340 **Girl in ethnic costume/Mädchen in Tracht**
1929/30, watercolor/Aquarell, 9 ³/₄ × 6 ¹/₂ in./250 × 165 mm
HM 55a

341 **Girls in ethnic costume/Mädchen in Tracht**
1929/30, watercolor/Aquarell, 11 ¹/₂ × 9 ¹/₄ in./290 × 235 mm
HM 196a

342

343

344

345

346

347

342 **Portrait of a boy/Porträt eines Knaben**
1929/30, watercolor/Aquarell, 10 $^1/_4$ × 7 in./260 × 178 mm
HM 128

343 **Portrait of a girl/Porträt eines Mädchens**
1929/30, watercolor/Aquarell, 10 $^1/_2$ × 7 $^1/_2$ in./269 × 188 mm
HM 129

344 **Boy, seated/Knabe, sitzend**
1929/30, watercolor/Aquarell, 15 $^3/_4$ × 9 $^3/_4$ in./400 × 250 mm
HM 238

345 **Young girl, seated/Mädchen, sitzend**
1929/30, watercolor, pencil/Aquarell, Bleistift,
16 $^1/_2$ × 9 $^1/_2$ in./420 × 243 mm
HM 236

346 **Child with a little dog/Kind mit kleinem Hund**
1929/30, charcoal, pastel chalk/Kohle, Pastell,
13 $^1/_2$ × 8 $^3/_4$ in./340 × 220 mm
HM 235

347 **Portrait of a woman/Porträt einer Frau**
1929/30, charcoal/Kohle, 10 $^1/_4$ × 7 $^1/_2$ in./262 × 190 mm
HM 141

348

349

351

350

352

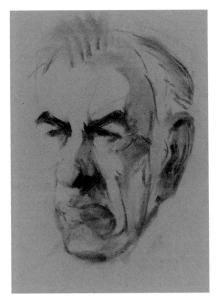

353

356

354

357

355

353 **Portrait of a man/Porträt eines Mannes**
1929/30, charcoal/Kohle, 9 $^1/_2$ × 6 $^1/_2$ in./240 × 165 mm
HM 152

354 **Portrait of a man/Porträt eines Mannes**
1929/30, graphite/Graphit, 10 × 7 in./255 × 180 mm
HM 855

355 **Portrait of a man/Porträt eines Mannes**
1929/30, graphite/Graphit, 11 $^1/_2$ × 9 in./295 × 228 mm
HM 929

356 **Portrait of a man with wide-brimmed hat/Porträt Mann mit Hut**
1929/30, pastel chalk/Pastell, 13 $^1/_4$ × 10 $^1/_2$ in./335 × 265 mm
HM 531

357 **Portrait of a man with wide-brimmed hat/Porträt Mann mit Hut**
1929/30, pastel chalk/Pastell, 9 $^3/_4$ × 7 in./250 × 175 mm
HM 883

358

358 **Portrait of a man/Porträt eines Mannes**
1929/36, charcoal/Kohle, 13 $^1/_2$ × 10 $^1/_4$ in./345 × 262 mm
HM 472

359 **Portrait of a man/Porträt eines Mannes**
1929/36, charcoal/Kohle, 10 × 6 $^3/_4$ in./251 × 174 mm
HM 880

360 **Two boys quarrelling/Zwei Buben, streitend**
1929/30, pencil/Bleistift, 2 $^3/_4$ × 4 in./70 × 100 mm
HM 64

361 **Peasant, standing/Bauer, stehend**
1929/30, watercolor/Aquarell, 19 $^3/_4$ × 12 $^3/_4$ in./502 × 327 mm
HM 938b

362 **Witch (design for a biscuit mould)/Die Hexe
(Entwurf für einen Model)**
1929/30, pencil/Bleistift, 4 × 4 $^1/_2$ in./101 × 112 mm
KS I

359

361

360

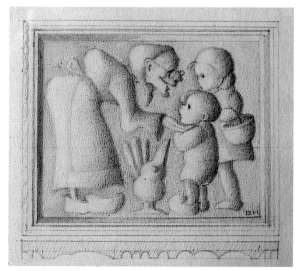

362

363

363 **Christ Child with Christmas-tree and cross/Christkind mit Christbaum und Kreuz**
1929/32, pen and ink/Tusche, 3 × 2 ¹/₂ in./74 × 64 mm
KS J

364 **Christ Child with angels in toy cart/Englein mit Christkind im Wägelchen**
1929/32, pen and ink/Tusche, 2 × 4 ¹/₂ in./48 × 108 mm
KS K

365 **Certificate, Simbach school 1930 (design)/Absolvia Simbach 1930 (Entwurf)**
1930, pencil/Bleistift, 3 ¹/₄ × 2 ¹/₂ in./80 × 63 mm
HM 447A

366 **Certificate, Simbach school 1930/Absolvia Simbach 1930**
1930, woodcut/Holzschnitt, 3 ¹/₄ × 2 ¹/₂ in./80 × 63 mm
HM 447B

364

365

366

367

367 Massing/Massing (Rundbild)
1930 datiert, oil/Öl, 15 ³/₄ in. diam./400 mm Durchm.
Privat

368 Portrait of Helene Angermaier/Porträt Helene Angermaier
1930, watercolor/Aquarell, 6 ¹/₂ × 5 ³/₄ in./164 × 147 mm
Privat

369 Peasant with hat/Bauer mit Hut
1930, watercolor/Aquarell, 19 ³/₄ × 12 ³/₄ in./502 × 327 mm
HM 938a

370 Lady in red/Dame in Rot
1930, watercolor, pencil/Aquarell, Bleistift,
19 ³/₄ × 11 in./500 × 280 mm
HM 239

371 Portrait of Professor Else Brauneis/Porträt Else Brauneis
1930, graphite/Graphit, 13 ³/₄ × 10 ³/₄ in./350 × 275 mm
KS L

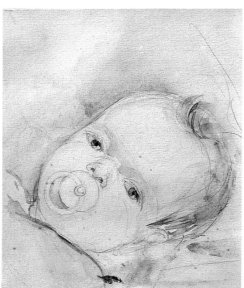

368

370

369

371

372

373

374

372 **Portrait of Professor Else Brauneis/Porträt Else Brauneis**
1930, watercolor, pencil/Aquarell, Bleistift,
10 $^3/_4$ × 7 $^1/_4$ in./270 × 187 mm
HM 142a

373 **Portrait of Professor Maximilian Dasio/Porträt Maximilian Dasio**
1930, watercolor/Aquarell, 10 $^3/_4$ × 8 $^1/_4$,89 in./270 × 208 mm
KS O

374 **Portrait of Professor Maximilian Dasio/Porträt Maximilian Dasio**
1930, graphite/Graphit, 10 $^1/_4$ × 7 in./260 × 180 mm
KS M

375 **Portrait of Professor Maximilian Dasio/Porträt Maximilian Dasio**
1930, pencil/Bleistift, 4 $^1/_4$ × 3 in./105 × 79 mm
KS N

376 **Portrait of Professor Maximilian Dasio, reading the
newspaper/Porträt Maximilian Dasio, Zeitung lesend**
1930, watercolor/Aquarell, 10 $^1/_2$ × 7 $^1/_2$ in./268 × 188 mm
HM 157

377 **Portrait of Professor Maximilian Dasio/Porträt Maximilian Dasio**
1930.03, woodcut/Holzschnitt, 4 $^1/_4$ × 2 $^3/_4$ in./105 × 70 mm
HM 636

375

376

377

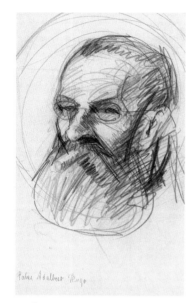

378

378 **Portrait of Father Adalbero Hugo/Porträt P. Adalbero Hugo**
1930, graphite/Graphit, 13 $^3/_4$ × 9 $^1/_4$ in./350 × 237 mm
HM 158

379 **Portrait of an old man/Porträt eines Greises**
1930, charcoal/Kohle, 15 $^3/_4$ × 10 $^1/_4$ in./400 × 260 mm
HM 229

380 **Portrait of Margret/Porträt Margret**
1930, graphite/Graphit, 11× 8 $^1/_4$ in./278 × 207 mm
KS P

381 **Portrait of Margret/Porträt Margret**
1930, charcoal/Kohle, 12 × 7 $^3/_4$ in./305 × 194 mm
HM 147

382 **Portrait of Margret/Porträt Margret**
1930, charcoal/Kohle, 10 $^3/_4$ × 8 $^1/_2$ in./270 × 217 mm
HM 148

379

381

380

382

383   384   385

386   388

387

383 **Margret, seated/Margret, sitzend**
1930, charcoal/Kohle, 11 × 7 in./280 × 175 mm
HM 200

384 **Margret, seated/Margret, sitzend**
1930, charcoal/Kohle, 12 $^1/_4$ × 6 $^1/_2$ in./310 × 165 mm
KS Q

385 **Margret, seated/Margret, sitzend**
1930, charcoal/Kohle, 12 $^3/_4$ × 7 in./326 × 180 mm
KS R

386 **Old man with peaked cap, seated/Alter Mann mit Mütze, sitzend**
1930, charcoal/Kohle, 14 $^1/_4$ × 8 $^3/_4$ in./363 × 223 mm
HM 945

387 **Old woman, seated/Alte Frau, sitzend**
1930, charcoal/Kohle, 12 $^3/_4$ × 8 $^1/_4$ in./322 × 207 mm
HM 947

388 **Portrait of an old man/Porträt eines alten Mannes**
1930, charcoal/Kohle, 9 $^3/_4$ × 7 in./250 × 176 mm
HM 881

389

392

390

393

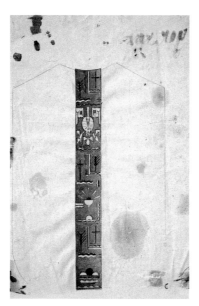

391

389 **Portrait of a woman/Porträt einer Frau**
1930, charcoal, pastel chalk/Kohle, Pastell,
11 $^1/_4$ × 7 $^3/_4$ in./285 × 198 mm
HM 138

390 **Portrait of Franz Hummel/Porträt Franz Hummel**
1930 dated/datiert, watercolor/Aquarell,
11 $^1/_4$ × 9 in./287 × 226 mm
HM 818

391 **Chasuble design (with symbolic pelican)/Messgewand-Entwurf
(mit Pelikan-Symbol)**
1930/31, watercolor, gilded bronze/Wasserfarbe, Goldbronze,
8 $^3/_4$ × 6 in./220 × 155 mm
HM 565

392 **Angel with flowers/Engel mit Blumen**
1931, pencil/Bleistift, 2 × 1 $^1/_4$ in./50 × 30 mm
HM 79

393 **Portrait of Centa Hummel/Porträt Centa Hummel**
1931.03, oil/Öl, 12 $^1/_2$ × 9 $^1/_2$ in./319 × 241 mm
HM 395

394

395

394 **Portrait of Adolf Hummel/Porträt Adolf Hummel mit Zigarre**
1931.03, pencil/Bleistift, 12 $\frac{1}{2}$ × 9 $\frac{1}{4}$ in./320 × 232 mm
HM 433

395 **Portrait of Franz Hummel/Porträt Franz Hummel**
1931.04, pencil/Bleistift, 13 $\frac{3}{4}$ × 10 in./351 × 252 mm
HM 819

396 **Wall hanging: Massing/Massing (Wandbehang)**
1931, appliqué/Applikation, 32 $\frac{3}{4}$ × 50 $\frac{3}{4}$ in./835 × 1290 mm
HM 493B

397 **Wall hanging: Massing (design)/**
Massing (Entwurf für Wandbehang)
1931, crayon/Farbstift, 4 $\frac{1}{4}$ × 6 $\frac{3}{4}$ in./110 × 174 mm
HM 493A

397

396

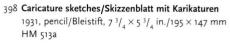

398

398 **Caricature sketches/Skizzenblatt mit Karikaturen**
1931, pencil/Bleistift, 7 $\frac{3}{4}$ × 5 $\frac{3}{4}$ in./195 × 147 mm
HM 513a

399 **Local gossips/Rottaler Bäuerinnen**
1931, pencil/Bleistift, 9 $\frac{1}{4}$ × 6 $\frac{3}{4}$ in./233 × 170 mm
HM 192

400 **Massing, cattle market/Massing, Viehmarkt**
1931, crayon, pencil/Farbstift, Bleistift,
8 $\frac{1}{4}$ × 11 $\frac{1}{4}$ in./210 × 285 mm
HM 885A

401 **Local characters/Rottaler Bauern**
1931, pencil/Bleistift, 9 $\frac{1}{4}$ × 6 $\frac{1}{2}$ in./235 × 165 mm
HM 193

402 **Massing, Corpus Christi Procession/Massing, Prozession**
1931, crayon, pencil/Farbstift, Bleistift,
8 $\frac{1}{4}$ × 10 $\frac{3}{4}$ in./210 × 270 mm
HM 886

399

401

400

402

Ausblick

Genaue Datierung und Entstehungsanlass folgender Bilder aus dem Jahr 1931 konnten nicht übereinstimmend festgelegt werden. Sie bieten allenfalls einen Ausblick auf das weitere Schaffen der Künstlerin.

View

It is not entirely certain when, and on what occasion, the following drawings dated from 1931 were done. At best, they offer a glimpse of Hummel's subsequent work.

403

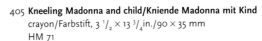

405

404

403 **Kneeling Madonna and child (sketch)/Kniende Madonna mit Kind (Skizze)**
pencil/Bleistift, 3 $^1/_2$ × 13 $^3/_4$ in./90 × 35 mm
HM 70

404 **Children's games/Beim Spiel**
pencil/Bleistift, 3 $^1/_4$ × 22 in./82 × 56 mm
HM 94

405 **Kneeling Madonna and child/Kniende Madonna mit Kind**
crayon/Farbstift, 3 $^1/_2$ × 13 $^3/_4$ in./90 × 35 mm
HM 71

406

407

408

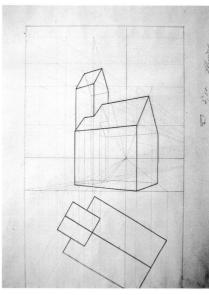

409

410

406 **Female nude, seated/Weiblicher Akt, sitzend**
charcoal/Kohle, 16 $^1/_4$ × 8 $^1/_4$ in./410 × 208 mm
HM 277

407 **Female nude, seated/Weiblicher Akt, sitzend**
charcoal/Kohle, 17 × 10 $^1/_4$ in./430 × 260 mm
HM 570

408 **Female nude, seated/Weiblicher Akt, sitzend**
charcoal/Kohle, 17 × 11 $^1/_4$ in./430 × 290 mm
HM 571

409 **Church (geometrical study)/Kirche – geometrische Figur**
pencil/Bleistift, 22 $^1/_2$ × 16 $^1/_2$ in./569 × 416 mm
HM 787b

410 **Dwarfs/Wichtelmännchen**
chalk/Kreide, 14 $^1/_2$ × 13 $^1/_2$ in./370 × 345 mm
HM 787a

Berta

Berta Hummel
1887.

Berta Hummel

Berta Hummel

B.H

B.HUMMEL

Hummel

H

Hummel B.

B Hummel

Berta Hummel 1931

Bibliography/Bibliographie

Hugo Schnell, Nekrolog. Innocentia Hummel, in: Das Münster 1, 1948, 4. Heft, 369

M. Gonsalva Wiegand OSF, Sketch me. Berta Hummel (Biography of Sister Maria Innocentia), St. Meinrad (Indiana) 1949, 2. Aufl. 1951

Eric Ehrman, Hummel. The complete collector's guide and illustrated reference, Huntington (New York) 1980

James S. Plaut, Formation of an Artist. The Early Works of Berta Hummel, Randolph (Massachusetts) 1980

Franz J. Tschudy, Leben und Werk der Schwester Maria Innocentia Hummel, in: 50 Jahre M. I. Hummel-Figuren 1935–1985, hrsg. vom Museum der Deutschen Porzellanindustrie Hohenberg/ Eger (Schriften und Kataloge des Museums der Deutschen Porzellanindustrie Bd. 5), Hohenberg/ Eger 1985

Christiane Vielhaber, M. I. Hummel-Figuren – Kleindenkmälder der Zeitgeschichte, in: 50 Jahre M. I. Hummel-Figuren 1935–1985, hrsg. vom Museum der Deutschen Porzellanindustrie Hohenberg/ Eger (Schriften und Kataloge des Museums der Deutschen Porzellanindustrie Bd. 5), Hohenberg/ Eger 1985

Die andere Berta Hummel. Unbekannte Werke einer bekannten Künstlerin, Ausstellungskatalog der Kunstsammlungen des Bistums Regensburg, Diözesanmuseum Regensburg (Kataloge und Schriften Bd. 3), München, Zürich 1986

Chronik der Familie Hummel, Massing (unveröffentlicht)

Kurt Flemig, Berta Hummel, in: ders., Karikaturisten-Lexikon, München, New Providence u. a. 1993, S. 127/28

Angelika Koller, Die Hummel, München 1994

Das Berta-Hummel-Museum im Hummelhaus, Ausstellungskatalog, Massing 1994

Letztes Schenken. Ausstellung zum 50. Todestag der Künstlerin Berta M. Innocentia Hummel, Massing 1996

Der Kreuzweg – Skizzen von M. Innocentia Hummel. Texte von M. Birgit Reutemann, Kloster Sießen 2000

Massing und Berta Hummel, Ausstellungskatalog, Massing 2000